First Aid
MANUAL

CW00670356

Frist Aid Kit

Items based on Risk Assessment for a small workplace	
First Aid Guidance or book	1
Contents List	1
Gloves Nitrile	4 pairs
Large Workplace Compliant Dressing	2
Medium Workplace Compliant Dressing	4
Conforming Bandages 7.5 cm x 4 M	2
Waterproof Sterile Plasters (Pack of 20) Blue for food	1
Eye Pad Dressing	2
Sterile Gauze Swabs 7.5 cm x 7.5 cm (1 x pack of five)	1
Non-Woven Triangular Bandage	2
Alcohol Free Cleansing Wipes	20
Cool Pack (Single use only)	1
Foil "silver" First Aid Blanket Adult	1
Roll of Microporous Tape	1
Pair of Scissors	1
Disposable Tweezers	2
Eye Wash/Wound Cleaning Pods 20 ml	5
Eye Wash bottle	1
Burn Dressing 10 cm x 10 cm	2
Low Adherent Dressing Pads 10 cm x 10 cm	2
Pocket Mask (For CPR) or Face Shield (For CPR)	1
Bag of 12 Safety Pins	1
Thermometer if looking after young children	1

Extra items for Major Trauma following Risk Assessment	Small Workplace
Tourniquet	1
Large Trauma Dressing	1
Haemostatic Dressing	1
Major Haemorrhage kits available from: **https://nativearb.co.uk/shop**	

Extra items for Outdoors following Risk Assessment	Small Workplace
Medi Wrap High Protection Blanket Medium or Large (Outdoors)	1
Survival Bag	1
Tick Removal Tool – Tick Card or Tick Tool	1
Vinegar for Wasps and Jellyfish	Some
Bicarbonate of soda for Bees, some research states it might also work on Nettles and Weaver Fish	Some

https://www.hse.gov.uk/simple-health-safety/firstaid/what-to-put-in-your-first-aid-kit.htm

First Aid Manual Forward

This manual has been produced after feedback from our clients asking for one simple to follow manual that covers all areas of First Aid. With a wide range of manuals on the market today, few cover all the basics required or are simple to follow, so to ensure our clients have a comprehensive point of reference for all things First Aid the content of this manual was put together by the team at Whitehorse and is based on their own practical experience of providing First Aid. It also follows the latest UK First Aid and NHS guidelines at the time of printing in relation to providing First Aid.

The Whitehorse team responsible for producing this comprehensive First Aid Manual

Robert Hamilton - 25 years Royal Navy, Mountain Leader, Kayak Instructor, 20 years experience in teaching First Aid, CertEd, NEBOSH Cert and a Paramedic.

Daniel Hamilton - L3 Forest School Leader, 12 years experience in teaching First Aid, DTLLS and an IHCD Ambulance Technician.

As well as running their own Ambulance Services providing medical teams to lots of high-risk events across the South of England for over 10 years they have also both worked for the NHS Ambulance Service as responders and front-line staff.

This First Aid Manual has been produced to fully comply with the following bodies:

- Resuscitation Council UK.
- The Health and Safety Executive (HSE).
- Early Years Foundation Stage.
- Forestry England (Forestry Commission).

The role of the Resuscitation Council UK in Workplace First Aid provision

They are the national expert in resuscitation who are working towards a day when every person in society has the skills they need to save a life.

Formed in 1983, they are committed to ensuring that survival rates for in and out of hospital cardiac arrest improve. They are doing this by using cutting edge research to help save lives by developing guidelines for members of the public and professionals to follow when administering First Aid in some of the following circumstances:

- Resuscitation of Adults, Children and Babies
- Choking of Adults, Children and Babies
- Use of AED
- Recovery Position

For more information on the most up to date guidelines 2021 go to www.resus.org

The role of the Health and Safety Executive (HSE) in workplace First Aid provision

First Aid at Work in the UK is controlled under "The Health and Safety (First Aid) Regulations 1981(Amended 2013)" produced by the Health and Safety Executive (HSE). It provides guidance to employers on their responsibilities.

As a minimum, a low-risk workplace such as a small office should have a First Aid box and a person appointed to take charge of First Aid arrangements, such as calling the emergency services if necessary.

Employers must also provide information about First Aid arrangements to their employees. Workplaces where there are more significant Health and Safety risks are more likely to need a trained First Aider.

The guidance helps employers make a First Aid needs assessment which will help employers decide what First Aid arrangements are appropriate for their workplace and help them to decide the appropriate level to which First Aiders should be trained.

A First Aider is someone who has undertaken training appropriate to the circumstances and should hold a valid certificate of competence in either:

- **First Aid at Work (FAW - 3 Days).**
- **Emergency First Aid at Work (EFAW - I Day).**
- **Other levels of training or qualifications that are appropriate to the circumstances, such as:**
  a. 12 Hr Paediatric First Aid.
  b. Basic Life Support.
  c. Immediate Life Support.
  d. 16 Hour Outdoor First Aid or Forest School First Aid.
  e. Forestry England extra training in special hazards classed as (+F).
  f. Use of extra equipment such as Oxygen as required.

Certificates for the purposes of First Aid at Work last for three years. Before their certificates expire, First Aiders will need to undertake a requalification course as appropriate, to obtain another three-year certificate. Once certificates have expired the First Aider is no longer considered to be competent to act as a workplace First Aider.

Can legal action be taken against First Aiders?

It is very unlikely that any action would be taken against a First Aider who was using the First Aid training they have received. However the HSE cannot give any specific advice on this issue as it does not fall within HSE's statutory powers. Therefore if you are worried it is recommended that you seek legal advice, or advice from your employer's insurance brokers on whether their policies cover First Aiders' liability.

Consent

It is important to gain consent before providing First Aid to someone with capacity, introduce yourself, tell them you are a First Aider and ask if you can help. If they don't have capacity or are unconscious you can act in the person's best interest.

The role of the Early Years Foundation Stage in workplace First Aid provision.

At least one person working in an Early Years setting must hold a current 12 Hour Paediatric First Aid (PFA) certificate and must be on the premises and available at all times when children are present, and must accompany children on outings.

Providers should take into account the number of children, staff, and layout of premises to ensure that a Paediatric First Aider is able to respond to emergencies quickly.

Providers must have and implement a policy, and procedures, for administering medicines. It must include systems for obtaining information about a child's needs for medicines, and for keeping this information up-to-date.

Training must be provided for staff where the administration of medicine requires medical or technical knowledge.

Prescription medicines must not be administered unless they have been prescribed for a child by a doctor, dentist, nurse or pharmacist (medicines containing aspirin should only be given if prescribed by a doctor).

Medicine, both prescription and non-prescription, must only be administered to a child where written permission for that particular medicine has been obtained from the child's parent and/or carer.

Providers must keep a written record each time a medicine is administered to a child, and inform the child's parents and/or carers on the same day, or as soon as reasonably practicable.

Forestry and responsibilities of a First Aider

First Aiders in Forest Services and Forestry England must hold a valid certificate of competence in either, First Aid at Work (FAW) (3 day), Emergency First Aid at Work (EFAW) (1 day) or Outdoor First Aid (2 day) .

However the above courses must include extra training in special hazards classed as (+F) which includes the following: Severe Chainsaw Cuts including Haemostatic Dressings and Tourniquets, Crush Injuries, Hypothermia and Lyme Disease.

Accident Recording and Reporting

The Reporting of Injuries, Diseases and Dangerous Occurrences Regulations 2013 (RIDDOR) is the law that requires employers, and other people in charge of work premises, to report and keep records of:

- Work-related accidents which cause deaths.
- Work-related accidents which cause certain serious (reportable) injuries.
- Diagnosed cases of certain industrial diseases.
- Certain 'dangerous occurrences' (incidents with the potential to cause harm).

An Accident Book is an essential document for employers and employees, who are required by law to record and report details of specified work-related injuries and incidents. First Aiders should ensure that they are aware of the location of the accident book and what information should be recorded in it.

Aims and Responsibilities of a First Aider

Never underestimate the importance of First Aid making a massive difference to the outcome for any ill or injured person.

A lot has been written over the years about the aims and responsibilities of a First Aider and the chain of survival, with the general consensus of most organisations involved in Pre Hospital Emergency Care being the 3 Ps.

First Aid Aims - The 3 Ps:

- Preserve Life.
- Prevent Worsening.
- Promote Recovery.

The Chain of Survival:

- Recognition of the requirement for cardiopulmonary resuscitation (CPR) and activation of the emergency response system.
- Early cardiopulmonary resuscitation (CPR) with an emphasis on good chest compressions.
- Early defibrillation.
- Advanced resuscitation by healthcare providers.

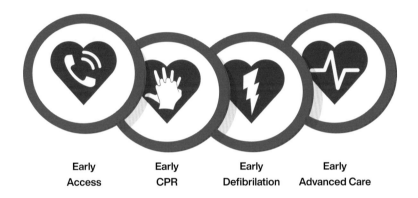

| Early | Early | Early | Early |
| Access | CPR | Defibrilation | Advanced Care |

First Aid Training

To ensure our students are given the best chance to learn and retain these skills we have tried to keep this manual as simple as possible to follow, with simple information on:

Conditions and History

Signs (Things you can see) **& Symptoms** (Things they tell you about)

Treatment

Our experience of delivering pre hospital care to ill and injured people in sometimes very remote locations or at high risk events, has taught us one thing:

" First Aid needs to be kept SIMPLE "

To keep it as simple as possible it is broken down into two main processes:

- The **Primary Survey** – The thing we should do first:
  Danger - Catastrophic Bleeding – Response – Airway – Breathing – Circulation

  (DOCTOR - A - B – C)
- The **Secondary Survey** – the thing we should do once happy with the Primary Survey: **History – Signs & Symptoms – Treatment.**

PRIMARY SURVEY

Remove Danger

If possible
If not **dial 999/112**

Do not take risks.

YES

DANGER?
Look for any danger.
Treat any catastrophic bleeding.

NO

Response?
Talk and gently shake or tap casualty

Alert Voice Physical Unresponsive

NO

Shout for Help!
Use speaker on mobile phone if possible to call help but don't leave the casualty yet or delay treatment.

YES

Secondary Survey

History
What has happened, medication, allergies & medical history.

Signs & Symptoms
How does the patient feel or look?
Check for bleeding, injuries and clues.
Try to work out what's wrong.

Treatment
Remember - if you're not sure, always seek professional medical advice.

Airway
Open the Airway by gently tilting the head back and lifting the chin.

B

Normal Breathing?
Look, listen and feel for no more than 10 seconds.

NO

Dial 999/112 Ask for AED

(On your own with a baby, child or drowning adult, resuscitate for 1 minute first).

YES

Maintain Airway

Place casualty in recovery position if:

- The casualty is vomiting or has fluid in airway
- You are by yourself
- If they are Pregnant make sure they are on their left side

Conduct a Secondary Survey

- Monitor airway and breathing
- Dial 999/112 if not already done

Circulation CPR
(Resuscitation)

30 - 2

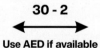

Use AED if available

- For a child, baby or drowning adult - give 5 initial breaths
- Give 30 chest compressions at 100-120 per minute, to a depth of 5 to 6 cm in an Adult, then give 2 rescue breaths if happy to do so, if not just continue good chest compressions. (For Children give compressions to a depth of 5 cm and Babies to a depth of 4 cm, roughly 1/3 the depth of chest).
- Continue giving cycles of compressions and rescue breaths and only stop CPR if: The casualty starts showing signs of life. An AED tells you not to touch the casualty. Ambulance crew tell you to stop. You are in danger or exhausted.
- If there is more than one rescuer try and chance over every 2 minutes with minimum interruption to good CPR.

PRIMARY SURVEY (**D**anger - **R**esponse – **A**irway – **B**reathing – **C**irculation)

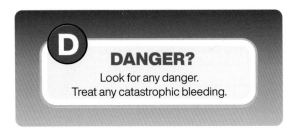

D **DANGER?**
Look for any danger.
Treat any catastrophic bleeding.

Consider your own safety and that of the person you are trying to help. Take a deep breath and give yourself a couple of seconds to take in the scene, look for dangers from things like:

- Vehicles.
- Car air bags.
- Fire.
- Animals.
- Falling branches.
- Slips & trips.
- Electricity.
- Cold water.
- Any others.

Check for and treat any **Catastrophic Haemorrhage** (Bleeding) (See page 75)

Electric Shock

If someone has had an electric shock it can cause internal and external burns and may cause cardiac arrhythmias and even lead to cardiac arrest.

DANGER
OVERHEAD
ELECTRIC POWER
LINES

Treatment of Electric Shock:

- Switch off the electrical current at the mains to break the contact between the person and the electrical supply.
- Do not go near or touch the person until you're sure the electrical supply has been switched off.
- If you can't reach the mains supply you need to remove any electrical appliance from the person by trying to use a dry wooden or plastic pole to move the item.
- Once the power supply has been switched off, conduct a Primary and Secondary survey.
- If conscious they should see a health care professional.
- If unconscious and breathing consider recovery position.
- If not breathing, Child start CPR (See page 20) Adult dial 999/112 for an ambulance and ask for location of nearest AED, then start CPR (See page 19)

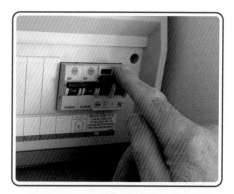

Outdoors High Voltage:

- High voltage electricity can jump over 8m and further when the air is damp, so great care must be taken around high voltage electricity outdoors, especially rail lines which may be electrified.
- Do not touch the person until you're sure the electrical supply has been switched off, remember wet wood conducts electricity.
- If in doubt don't approach casualty. Call 999/112 and ask for Fire Service.
- If a vehicle is in contact with electricity the occupants should stay in the vehicle if safe to do so.
- Once the power supply has been switched off follow above guidance.

Danger
Do not touch
the live rail

Response – Consciousness

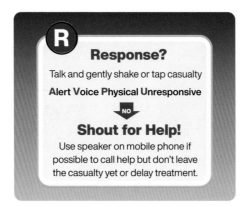

R

Response?

Talk and gently shake or tap casualty

Alert Voice Physical Unresponsive

NO

Shout for Help!

Use speaker on mobile phone if possible to call help but don't leave the casualty yet or delay treatment.

A – **Alert** – Person appears alert – Move to Secondary Survey.

V – **Voice** - Try and gain a response by voice, talking into both ears, ask if they are alright, try clapping your hands, if unresponsive move to "P".

P – **Pain/Physical** - Try to get a response through physical contact by tapping or gently shaking their shoulders. For Babies tap feet and check grip.

U – **Unresponsive** - If no response from "P" assume unconsciousness and shout for help but don't leave person if the person appears unresponsive.

Airway

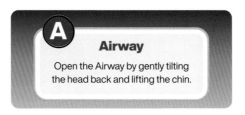

A

Airway

Open the Airway by gently tilting the head back and lifting the chin.

Various things can affect a person's airway and then quickly effect their ability to breathe normally with the knock-on effect of reducing their blood oxygen to dangerous levels, so the importance of First Aiders opening a person's airway should not be understated.

The following are some of the things that can affect a person's airway:

Choking on food or objects - Vomit - Fluids - Swelling - Trauma - Burns Strangulation - Hanging - Helmets - The persons own tongue

(If you suspect choking see pages 26 to 31 for procedure)

The most common is a person's own tongue

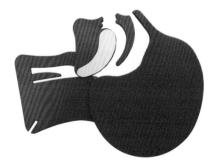

Tongue blocking Airway   Chin lift and Tongue removed from Airway

It is extremely important that if there's no response, leave the person in the position they're in and open their airway. If this is not possible in the position they're in, gently turn them onto their back and then open their airway (See page 38).

If you see fluids, sick or mud in their mouth you may need to turn the person on their side to clear the mouth before you open the airway (See pages 35 to 37) However the RC(UK) don't want this to delay opening the Airway.

Open the airway by placing one hand on the forehead and gently tilt their head back, use your other hand to lift the tip of the chin using 2 fingers and pull forward to open mouth fully. This should move the tongue away from the back of the throat. Be careful not to push on the floor of the mouth, as this will push the tongue upwards and can obstruct the airway.

Use a jaw thrust technique if you suspect a spinal injury (See page 13).

Remember: Airway is a primary survey issue, whereas spinal injury is secondary.

Helmet Removal Technique

There is always discussion about "should I remove a helmet?". Keep it simple, if person is unresponsive and you can't check their airway or you are not sure they are breathing normally because of a helmet. You should remove it.

Rescuer 1 should grab each side of the helmet with fingers griping the rim if possible.

Rescuer 2 should cut or undo chin strap, place one hand under the neck and the other hand on the chin as shown.

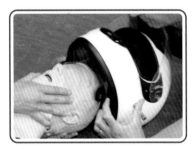

Rescuer 2 then supports the head.

Rescuer 1 moves the helmet forward to back, not side to side. Once clear checks it for damage and checks head for injuries.

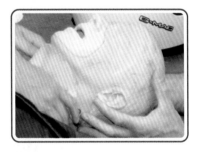

Rescuer 1 then takes over and supports the head as show.

Rescuer 2 can then check airway and breathing as required.

Use a jaw thrust technique if you suspect a spinal injury. Place your hands on either side of their head and use your fingertips to gently lift the angle of the jaw forward and upwards, without moving the head.

Jaw Thrust Technique

Remember: Airway is a primary survey issue, whereas spinal injury is secondary.

Breathing

B

Normal Breathing?

Look, listen and feel for no more than 10 seconds.

NO

Dial 999/112 Ask for AED

(On your own with a baby, child or drowning adult, resuscitate for 1 minute first).

How We Breathe:

Our body has sensors by our heart and in our brain which monitor the CO_2 in our blood supply. As the CO_2 rises the brain will send signals to our main breathing muscle, our diaphragm, as muscles contract and relax, so the diaphragm contracts to draw air in and relaxes to release air

The fact the diaphragm only operates in is a major problem when it comes to our tongue or choking, as when our airway is blocked by these the CO_2 level in our body goes up and the brain in turn tells the diaphragm to work harder, thus pulling the tongue or choking object further into their airway, further reducing their blood oxygen to dangerous levels.

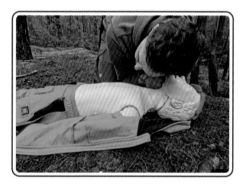

Check breathing for no more than 10 seconds

To check if a person is still breathing normally:

- Make sure the airway is open.
- **LOOK** to see if their abdomen is pulling in and their chest is rising and falling.
- Place you ear by their mouth and nose and **LISTEN** for normal breathing sounds.
- Try and **FEEL** their breath against your cheek for no more than 10 seconds.
- Consider expected breathing rates for age.

If they're breathing normally, move to the secondary survey and consider placing them in the recovery position so their airway remains clear of obstructions.

Gasping, noisy or irregular breathing is not normal breathing and it could be **Agonal Gasping** which is common in the first few minutes after a sudden cardiac arrest. Agonal breathing is sudden, irregular gasps of breath which must not be mistaken for normal breathing,

For an Adult that isn't breathing or is not breathing normally, call 999/112 for an ambulance, ask for the nearest AED and begin Resuscitation,(See page 19)

For a Baby, Child or a Drowning Adult that isn't breathing or is not breathing normally begin Resuscitation (See pages 20 or 21) for one minute then call 999/112 for an ambulance, ask for the nearest AED and return to Resuscitation.

Breathing Rates:

Baby 0 to 1 year
40 to 25 per minute

Child 1 to 18 years
25 to 16 per minute

Adult 18 years up
12 to 16 per minute

What We Breathe:

We inhale:

78%	Nitrogen
21%	Oxygen
0.04%	Carbon Dioxide
1%	Other Gases

We exhale:

78%	Nitrogen
16.4%	Oxygen
4.4%	Carbon dioxide
1%	Other Gases

As we only use a small amount of the Oxygen we inhale we can use the exhaled Oxygen to perform mouth to mouth rescue breaths to good effect.

Circulation

Circulation CPR (Resuscitation)

30 - 2

⟵⟶

Use AED if available

- For a child, baby or drowning adult - give 5 initial breaths
- Give 30 chest compressions at 100-120 per minute, to a depth of 5 to 6 cm in an Adult, then give 2 rescue breaths if happy to do so, if not just continue good chest compressions. (For Children give compressions to a depth of 5 cm and Babies to a depth of 4 cm, roughly 1/3 the depth of chest).
- Continue giving cycles of compressions and rescue breaths and only stop CPR if: The casualty starts showing signs of life. An AED tells you not to touch the casualty. Ambulance crew tell you to stop. You are in danger or exhausted.
- If there is more than one rescuer try and chance over every 2 minutes with minimum interruption to good CPR.

The cardiovascular system delivers nutrients and oxygen to all the cells in the body. It consists of the heart and the blood vessels running through the entire body with the arteries carrying blood away from the heart and the veins carrying it back to the heart.

The following conditions can affect the blood pressure:

- Shock (See Pages 32-33).
- Fainting. (See Page 34).
- Anaphylaxis. (See Pages 40-41).
- Heart Attack. (See Pages 48-49).
- Cardiac Arrest. (See Page 51).
- Hypothermia. (See Pages 68-69).
- Heat Exhaustion. (See Page 70).
- External and Internal Bleeding. (See Pages 72-97).
- Burns. (See Pages 104-105).
- Vomiting and Diarrhoea.

Normal Resting Heart Rates:

Baby 0 to 1 year
160-110 beats per minute

Child 1 to 18 years
110-60 beats per minute

Adult 18 up
55-90 beats per minute

Circulatory System

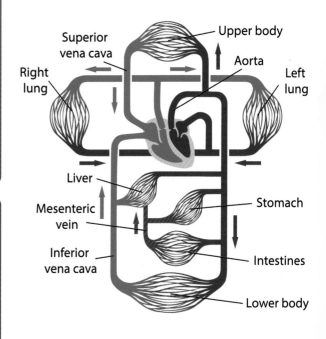

We can check for good circulation and blood pressure by checking for capillary refill and taking a pulse.

To check Capillary Refill:

- Apply finger pressure by squeezing the nail bed of either a finger or toe or by applying finger pressure on the forehead or sternum.
- Apply pressure for around 5 seconds.
- Release pressure and capillaries should refill within 3 seconds.
- Any longer could indicate reduced circulation.

How to check a pulse:

Use the below techniques to count how many times the heart beats in 1 minute (60 seconds) also consider how strong it feels.

To find a pulse in someone's wrist: (Radial Pulse)

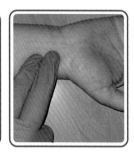

- Hold out their hand, palm facing upwards.
- Press your first (index) finger and middle finger on the inside of their wrist, at the base of their thumb – don't use your thumb as it has its own pulse.
- Press their skin lightly until you can feel their pulse – if you can't find it, try pressing a little harder or move your fingers around.

To find a pulse in someone's neck: (Carotid Pulse)

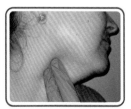

- Press your first finger and middle finger to the side of their neck, just under their jaw and beside their windpipe – don't use your thumb.
- Press their skin lightly to feel their pulse – if you can't find it, try pressing a bit harder or move your fingers around.

To find a pulse in an upper arm, especially in babies: (Brachial Pulse)

- Straighten the arm if possible.
- Use the pads of at least two of your fingers to push the muscle near the elbow over slightly from the inside of arm, move your fingers around slightly to locate the pulse, you may have to press firmly.

The Principles of Cardio Pulmonary Resuscitation (CPR)

The theory behind providing CPR is to maintain blood pressure and oxygen saturation until the person can do it for themselves or an Automatic External Defibrillation (AED) or medical assistance arrives. Research shows the time between Breathing stopping or Cardiac Arrest occurring and CPR starting is critical to survival and if not started in the first 10 minutes the outcomes are poor and with every minute CPR is not started, survival chance goes down by around 10%. In Cardiac Arrest it also showed if an AED is not used within 10 Minutes, survival rates are very poor.

Chest Compressions manually operate the heart providing blood pressure in the circulation system to allow the blood to oxygenate tissues and organs and also remove CO_2 through the lungs. They should be performed on a firm surface whenever feasible.

Chest Compression Only CPR for adult resuscitation, if you are unsure about giving rescue breaths just maintain chest compressions.

Adult Compressions should be delivered on the lower half of the sternum (Centre of the chest) by positioning yourself arms straight and vertically above the person's chest, push to a depth of at least 5 cm but not more than 6 cm, at a rate of 100–120 min allowing the chest to recoil completely after each compression with few interruptions. (See opposite)

Child and Baby Compressions should be delivered on the lower half of the sternum (Breastbone), roughly one fingers width up from end of sternum avoiding upper abdomen. Use thumbs or two fingers for baby under 1 year and the heel of one hand for child over 1 year. Push to a depth of at least one-third of the chest, roughly 4 cm for baby and 5 cm for child at a rate of 100–120 min with few interruptions. (See pages 20-21)

Rescue Breaths are designed to provide oxygen directly into a patient's lungs ready to be picked up by the circulation system.

The big question is always which one should I do first?

For Adults over 18 years the most common reason CPR is required is the heart (The Pump) failing, dropping the blood pressure and oxygen flow. They may still have oxygen in the system, just not being pumped round, so getting the pump working is the priority, so an AED and Chest Compressions are the priority (See page 19 Adult CPR)

For Babies, Children up to the age of 18 years and Drowning Adults the most common reason CPR is required will be lack of oxygen to the tissue caused by a respiratory condition dropping the oxygen levels and increasing the CO_2 levels in the blood. Their heart could still be working but will fail as hypoxia increases, so getting oxygen into their system with rescue breaths before the heart stops is the priority for a good outcome. These should even come before getting help if this would delay giving them CPR (See pages 20 and 21 Child/Baby CPR).

Adult (18+) Resuscitation

If an adult is Not Breathing normally or has Noisy Breathing (Agonal Gasps) dial 999/112 and ask for nearest AED.

If AED available use it first, if not available then start Resuscitation.

Give 30 Chest Compressions by linking your hands together and placing the heal in the centre of their chest as shown below.

Position for chest compressions

Heal of hand position for 30 chest compressions

You should aim to push to a depth of at least 5 cm, but not more than 6 cm, roughly 1/3 of the chest at a rate of 100-120 beats a minute (2 a second) (30 in 15 seconds).

Then give rescue breaths if happy to do so by closing their nose by pinching with one hand while opening and maintaining their airway with your other hand.

Open your mouth fully and seal your lips around theirs.

Give 1 rescue breath, over 1 second checking to see if chest rises, take your face away while watching for chest falling, take a fresh breath and repeat up to a maximum of 2 rescue breaths.

Give 2 rescue breaths

If you are not sure about giving rescue breaths just maintain effective chest compressions.

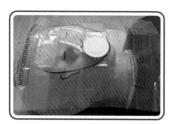 

Consider using a face shield or pocket mask when giving Rescue Breaths

Repeat 30 Chest Compressions and 2 Rescue Breaths until help or AED arrives, you are too tired or they show signs of breathing.

Child CPR

If a child or drowning adult is Not Breathing normally or has Noisy Breathing (Agonal Gasps) it is important to give 5 rescue breaths first.

Give rescue breaths by closing their nose by pinching with one hand while opening and maintaining their airway with your other hand.

Open your mouth fully and seal your lips around theirs.

Give 1 rescue breath, over 1 second checking to see if chest rises, take your face away while watching for chest falling, take a fresh breath and repeat up to a maximum of 5 rescue breaths.

Position for chest compressions

If you have difficulty achieving an effective breath, check for and remove any visible obstruction, do not perform a blind finger sweep. Try repositioning the head to open the airway. Make up to 5 attempts to achieve effective breaths.

If no response from the rescue breaths give 30 Chest Compressions by placing one or two hands as required, heal first in the centre of their chest as shown below.

 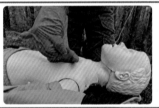 

Heal of hand position for chest compressions

With the heel of your hand as show above you should aim to push to a depth of 5 cm or 1/3 of chest at a rate of 100-120 beats a minute (2 a second) (30 in 15 seconds).

Then give a further 2 Rescue Breaths and repeat 30 Chest Compressions to 2 Rescue Breaths for 1 minute then Dial 999/112 and ask for nearest AED if not already done.

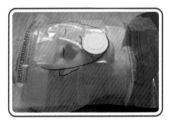 

Consider using a face shield or pocket mask when giving Rescue Breaths

Repeat 30 Chest Compressions and 2 Rescue Breaths until help or AED arrives, you are too tired or they show signs of breathing.

Baby Resuscitation

It is important when checking for breathing in babies that we don't move the head back to much as this can close the airway, natural alignment as show should be used.

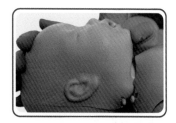

If a Baby is Not Breathing normally, it is important to give 5 rescue breaths first.

Give rescue breaths while maintaining their airway with neutral alignment.

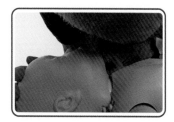

Open your mouth fully and seal your lips around their mouth and nose, consider using a Face Shield or Pocket Mask.

Give 1 rescue breath, over 1 second checking to see if chest rises, take your face away while watching for chest falling, take a fresh breath and repeat up to a maximum of 5 rescue breaths.

If you have difficulty achieving an effective breath, check for and remove any visible obstruction, do not perform a blind finger sweep, also reposition head to ensure airway is open. Make up to 5 attempts to achieve effective breaths.

If no response from the rescue breaths give 30 Chest Compressions by placing your fingers as required in the centre of their chest as shown below.

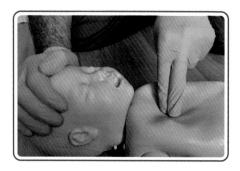 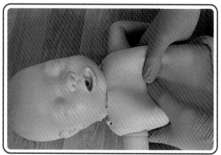

Give Chest Compressions with fingers or thumbs for small babies

With two finger or thumbs as show above you should aim to push to a depth of 4 cm or 1/3 of chest at a rate of 100-120 beats a minute (2 a second) (30 in 15 seconds).

Repeat 30 Chest Compressions and 2 Rescue Breaths until help or AED arrives, you are too tired or they show signs of breathing.

Automatic External Defibrillator (AED)

An AED is a medical device used in the treatment of sudden Cardiac Arrest (See page 51). They are designed for easy use with no training required as it talks the rescuer through each step. Obtainable from shops, businesses or by ringing 999/112 who will give the location of the nearest one.

It is a normal misconception that an AED will start a heart, however the opposite is true, it does in fact stop the heart in the hope the heart's own pacemaker electrical signal can restart the heart back into Normal Sinus Rhythm (NSR).

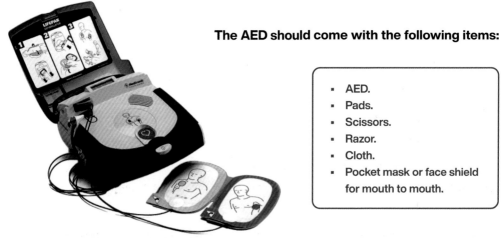

The AED should come with the following items:

- AED.
- Pads.
- Scissors.
- Razor.
- Cloth.
- Pocket mask or face shield for mouth to mouth.

Child Pads

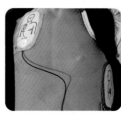

Adults Pads

Dual Pads

How to use an AED:

- If CPR is in progress, work round the person doing CPR to reduce the time of no compressions.
- If lone rescuer use the AED first.
- Open AED, follow the prompts, (some need turning on).
- Clear chest by removing clothing including bras and jewellery.
- Shave hair from pad location if required.
- Dry chest before applying pads.
- Once pads are applied the AED will ask you to stand clear while it analysis.

Applying Pads:

- Adult pads should be applied as per the diagrams on them (See page 22).
- Child (Under 8 years) or dual pads should be applied as per the diagram on them, on the front and back of chest (See page 22).
- If you think the patient has a pacemaker fitted in the pad position, try applying the pads as close to the indicated site as possible without covering the pacemaker, or place one front and one back of chest.

If the AED identifies Ventricular Fibrillation (VF) (See page 51) it will say "Shock Advised" it will advise the rescuer to stay clear and either get the rescuer to push a shock button or it may shock autonomously with no requirement for rescuer to push a button. Once shock delivered it will ask rescuer to commence CPR.

If the AED identifies either Normal Sinus Rhythm (NSR) (See page 51) or Asystole (Flat line) (See page 51) it will say "No Shock Advised" and it will advise the rescuer to start CPR if required. Before starting CPR just check if the person is breathing or not.

If an AED is being used for an extended time it will re-analyse every 2 minutes, asking the rescuer to stand clear while it re-analysis.

If a community AED has been used and finished with, it should be put back in the box it came from and re-locked. The custodian will be advised by the Ambulance Service that it has been used and they will check it and return to service.

To see if there is an AED near you, go to: www.thecircuit.uk
If you want to register your own AED as public access, go to: www.defibfinder.uk

SECONDARY SURVEY

1

Keep patient calm and still then check History:
What has happened?
Are they on any medication?
Do they have any medical conditions?
Do they have any allergies?
When did they last eat or drink anything?
Check for Medical alert bracelets, medical ID
on mobile phone etc
Are there any witnesses?
Survey scene: any ladders, equipment, animals,
vehicles, water, electricity etc

2

Check head, neck and back for:
Airway issues (blockages and swelling)
Bruising (especially behind ears and around eyes)
Swelling
Open wounds
Fluid leaking from ears and nose
Headaches, dizziness or blurred vision
Any Pain (gently palpate neck)
Confusion or memory loss
Sweaty/Clammy
Facial colour (pale, purple, blue, flushed)
(IF THERE IS NECK OR BACK PAIN
SUPPORT THE HEAD AND KEEP THE
PATIENT STILL DIAL 999)

3

Check the shoulders and chest
Ask the patient to take a deep breath:
Is there equal rise and fall?
Is there any pain or difficulty breathing?
Is the breathing fast or slow, check rate?
Check the area for bruising and wounds
Do they have any type of chest pain?
Compare collar bones for signs of fractures

6

Check arms and hands
Can the patient move both arms?
Can the patient move their fingers?
Does the patient have any pain?
Check for bleeding
Check for deformity
Check for swelling and bruising
Check fingertips for circulation
Check radial pulse if trained to do so

4

Check abdomen and pelvis
Check for any bruising
Check for any abnormality
Gently palpate abdomen for pain
Check for incontinence
Check for bleeding

(DO NOT squeeze or rock pelvis)

5

Check both legs and feet
Can the patient move both legs?
Can the patient move their toes?
Does the patient have any pain?
Check for bleeding
Check for deformity
Check for swelling and bruising
Take off shoes and socks then check
circulation

7

Treatment
Treat any medical conditions
Keep patient comfortable & consider recovery position
Treat any injuries
Consider Shock, lay Patient down and raise legs
If needed dial 999/112
Keep patient warm or cool depending on situation
Re check any wound dressings
Re check any burns and cool for longer if needed

Hypoxia

Hypoxia is caused by low levels of oxygen in your body tissues. Most conditions that cause breathing difficulties can put a person at risk for hypoxia.

The body's response to Hypoxia:

If the body detects low levels of oxygen in the blood, adrenaline/epinephrine is released which will cause the following to happen.

- Increase the heart rate.
- Increase the strength of the heart beat (and blood pressure).
- Divert blood away from the skin, intestines and stomach.
- Divert blood towards the heart, lungs, and brain.
- Dilate the air passages in the lungs (bronchioles).

Signs and Symptoms:

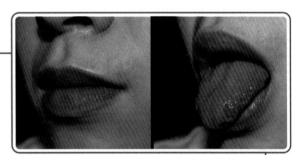

- Pale clammy skin.
- Increased pulse rate.
- Weakening of the pulse.
- Nausea and/or vomiting.
- Increased respiratory rate (caused by oxygen deficiency).
- Blue tinges to the skin and lips (cyanosis) look inside mouth and at tongue on darker skin.
- Confusion or dizziness.
- Reducing levels of consciousness.
- Clues from the cause of the hypoxia (i.e. bleeding, injury, chest pain etc).

Treatment:

- Remove or treat the cause of the hypoxia (if possible).
- Maintain airway and breathing.
- Sit person down but keep sat upright, if you suspect heavy blood loss treat for shock.
- If unconscious, check Airway and Breathing, if breathing place in recovery position.
- Ring 999/112 for assistance.
- If not breathing or unsure start resuscitation.

Choking

Choking is caused by breathing in either food or an object. To reduce the risk from food we should chew our food with our mouth closed, no talking whilst eating,

Food Standards Agency don't recommend the following foods be given to under 5 year olds due to the high risk of choking:

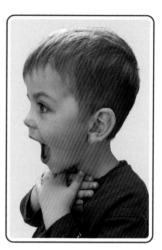

- Ice Cubes.
- Chewing Gum.
- Marshmallows.
- Peanut Butter.
- Nuts.
- Popcorn.
- Jelly Cubes.
- Boiled Sweets.
- Raisins.
- Other Dried Fruits.

As mentioned before the main problem with Choking is the diaphragm only operating on the way in, thus when their airway is blocked by an object the CO2 level in our body goes up and the brain in turn tells the diaphragm to work harder, thus pulling the choking object further into their airway, further reducing their blood oxygen to dangerous levels.

In adults we can use our abdominal muscles to produce an effective cough which might help push the diaphragm up helping to expel air and clear the airway. However young children don't have developed abdominal muscles so coughing will not be as effective.

Signs and Symptoms:

- The signs and symptoms of choking usually develop quickly and get rapidly worse.
- The person will not be able to talk or make any sounds.
- They may have a flushed face to start with then rapidly becoming blue (Hypoxic) harder to see on dark skin.
- They may be grasping at their throat.
- They may look and act distressed.
- Young children may become quiet and even hide from view.
- Babies will become quite and quickly becoming blue (Hypoxic).
- They may become unconscious.

www.food.gov.uk/sites/default/files/media/document/Early%20Years%20Choking%2 Hazards%20Poster_English.pdf

www.foundationyears.org.uk/files/2021/09/Early-Years-Choking-Hazards-Table_FINAL_21-Sept-2021.pdf

Adult Choking

- Ask, are you choking?
- Get them to open their mouth.
- Encourage coughing.

Encourage coughing

- If not clear, lean them forward.
- Support their chest and give 1 back blow with the heel of your free hand between their shoulders.
- If not clear repeat up to a maximum of 5 blows.
- If still not clear Ring 999/112.

Give up to 5 back blows

- Give 1 abdominal thrust, by making a fist with one hand placed in the persons abdomen just under the lower ribs, grasp your fist and pull sharply in and upwards.
- If not clear repeat up to a maximum of 5 thrusts.

Hand position for abdo thrusts

- If not clear repeat 5 back blows, then 5 abdominal thrusts until airway is clear or they become unconscious.

Give up to 5 abdo thrusts

- If they become unconscious and their airway still appears blocked, ring 999/112 back if required and start Adult CPR (See page 19).
- If available and you are trained consider using a LifeVac Anti-Choking device (See page 31)

Repeat both as required

Large Person Choking

- If dealing with a large person who you can't get your arms round, try the coughing and back blows first.
- If not working ring 999/112 and get them to lie on their back, sit astride their legs, lock your hands together and place the heel into the persons abdomen just under the lower ribs and push up into the abdomen up to 5 times, you are trying to push the diaphragm up like a normal abdominal thrust.
- If possible, also turn them on their side and try 5 more back blows.
- If they become unconscious and their airway still appears blocked Ring 999/112 back if required and start Adult CPR (See page 19).
- If available and you are trained consider using a LifeVac Anti-Choking device (See page 31).

Pregnant Person Choking

- If dealing with a pregnant person, try the coughing and back blows first.
- If that does not work get them to lie on their back and try chest compressions.
- If they become unconscious and their airway still appears blocked Ring 999/112 back if required and start Adult CPR (See page 19).
- If available and you are trained consider using a LifeVac Anti-Choking device (See page 31).

Choking On Your Own

- Call 999/112 preferably from a land line and leave phone off the hook, same procedure for a mobile. The operator should take action to trace the call.
- Try to cough the obstruction out at the same time as trying to find someone to help.
- You could try tapping "Save Our Souls" (SOS) with 3 short taps... 3 long taps --- 3 short taps ... if time allows.
- Find a suitable sturdy object like a chair or table that you can push against.
- Place a fist into your abdomen just under the lower ribs, grasp your fist with your free hand, then place against the object and push sharply in and upward.
- Repeat this process until object comes out, help arrives or you become unconscious.
- If available and you are trained consider using a LifeVac Anti-Choking device (See page 31).
- If you can remove the object, pick up phone and talk to operator.
- Then seek medical help as required.

Child Choking

- Ask, are you choking?
- Get them to open their mouth.
- Encourage coughing.

Encourage coughing

- If not clear, lean them forward.
- Either support their chest or place over your knee and give 1 back blow with the heel of your free hand between their shoulders.
- If not clear repeat up to a maximum of 5 blows.

Give up to 5 back blows standing

- If still not clear Ring 999/112.
- Give 1 abdominal thrust, by making a fist with one hand placed in the Child's abdomen just under the lower ribs, grasp your fist and pull sharply in and upwards.
- If not clear repeat up to a maximum of 5 thrusts.

or give up to 5 back blows over your knee

- If not clear repeat 5 back blows, then 5 abdominal thrusts. until airway is clear or they become unconscious.
- If unconscious check mouth for foreign bodies, if any present attempt to remove with a single finger sweep.
- NO blind or repeated finger sweeps as this can push the object deeper into the airway.

Give up to 5 abdo thrusts

- If still appears blocked, ring 999/112 back if required and Start Child CPR (See page 20).
- If available and you are trained consider using a LifeVac Anti-Choking device (See page 31)

Repeat both as required

Baby Choking

- Look in their mouth.
- If coughing it could just be a partial obstruction, turn them on their side head down and check to see if it clears.

Give up to 5 back blows

- If silent lay them on their front along one of your arms with their face down. With the palm and fingers give a back blow between the shoulders.
- Check to see if airway has cleared.
- If not repeat up to a maximum of 5 back blows.
- If still not clear Ring 999/112.
- **DO NOT GIVE ABDOMINAL THRUSTS TO BABIES.**

- Turn baby over and lay them along your arm face up slightly tilted to the side.
- With 2 fingers or the flat of your hand positioned in the centre of their chest, give a chest thrust.

Give up to 5 chest thrusts
with 2 fingers

- Check to see if airway has cleared.
- If not repeat up to a maximum of 5 chest thrusts.

- Repeat 5 back blows then 5 chest thrusts, until airway is clear or they become unconscious.

- If unconscious check mouth for foreign bodies, if any present attempt to remove with a single finger sweep.
- NO blind or repeated finger sweeps as this can push the object deeper into the airway.

Or use the flat of your hand

- If still appears blocked, ring 999/112 back if required and Start Baby CPR (See page 21).
- If available and you are trained consider using a LifeVac Anti-Choking device (See page 31).

Repeat both as required

LifeVac Anti-Choking Device for Airway Clearance

The UK Medicines and Healthcare products Regulatory Agency (MHRA) warns the public not to buy unbranded devices as they do not comply with device regulations and could cause harm. They have worked with LifeVac to ensure their device instructions clearly explain its intended purpose and continue to recommend that users follow the established Basic Life Support protocols in the UK first.

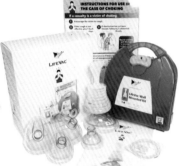

The Resuscitation Council UK do not currently support their use, as there is insufficient research and evidence on the safety or effectiveness of these devices. They are concerned that the use of these devices could delay established treatments for choking.

So we highly recommended that you receive training before using a LifeVac device.

LifeVac is a single use lifesaving apparatus developed to help clear the airway in a choking victim due to a Foreign Body Airway Obstruction.

Only to be used - **WHEN STANDARD BASIC LIFE SUPPORT FOR CHOKING HAS BEEN FOLLOWED WITHOUT SUCCESS** or **CANNOT BE APPLIED** because any of the following apply: Person in a wheelchair, bedridden, sitting at a table, pregnant or obese. (This is not an exhaustive list).

EASY AS

① PLACE ② PUSH ③ PULL

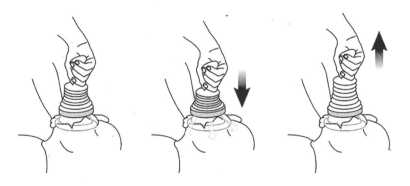

For more information and detailed instructions on its use, please go to www.lifevac.uk or email info@lifevac.uk   https://www.gov.uk/guidance/medical-devices-information-for-users-and patients https://www.resus.org.uk/about-us/news-and-events/rcuks-position-use-suction-based-airway-clearance-devices-choking-individuals

Shock

In the case of a serious injury or illness, it's important to look out for signs of shock. Shock is a life-threatening condition that occurs when the circulatory system fails to provide enough oxygenated blood to the body and, as a result, deprives the vital organs of oxygen.

This is usually the result of severe blood loss, but it can also occur after severe burns, severe vomiting, a heart attack, a bacterial infection, or a severe allergic reaction (anaphylaxis).

The type of shock described here isn't the same as the **Emotional Shock** the response of feeling shocked, which can also occur after an accident. Refer to bottom of page 33.

Signs and Symptoms:

- Pale, cold and clammy skin, much harder to see on dark skin.
- Sweating.
- Rapid, shallow breathing.
- Weakness and dizziness.
- Feeling sick and possibly vomiting.
- Thirst.
- Yawning.
- Sighing.

Types of Shock:

Cardiogenic:
Heart problems like, Heart Attack, Cardiac Arrest and Mechanical or Electrical faults.

Anaphylactic:
Life threatening allergic reaction.

Hypovolaemic:
Low blood volume caused by Fainting, External and Internal Bleeding, Burns, Heat Exhaustion, Vomiting and Diarrhoea.

Treatment:

- Treat any obvious injuries.
- Lie the person down if their injuries allow you to and, if possible, raise and support their legs.
- Use a coat or blanket to keep them warm.
- Do not give them anything to eat or drink, a sip of water is ok to wet their dry mouth.
- Give them lots of comfort and reassurance.
- If their condition does not improve seek medical help by ringing 999/112.
- If unconscious, check Airway and Breathing, if breathing place in recovery position.
- If not breathing or unsure Ring 999/112 back and start resuscitation.

Emotional Shock:

Consider people might be suffering from Emotional Shock during or after an event and give them the following advice if required:

- Sit down and give yourself time.
- Talk about the event.
- Speak to others that have experienced the same thing as you.
- Ask for support.
- Avoid spending lots of time alone.
- Stick to your routine.
- Consider seeking professional help.
- Notice how you're feeling.

Fainting

Fainting is when a person passes out for a short time normally due to low blood pressure. It's not usually a sign of something serious, but if it happens regularly, you should seek medical advice.

Causes:

- Standing up too quickly – this could be a sign of low blood pressure.
- Not eating or drinking enough.
- Eating a large meal then going into rest and digest mode (Common in the elderly).
- Being too hot.
- Being very upset, witnessing something like an accident, being angry or in severe pain.
- Heart problems.
- Taking drugs or too much alcohol.

Signs and Symptoms:

- Fainting usually happens suddenly.
- Dizziness.
- Pale, cold and clammy skin, much harder to see on dark skin.
- Slurred speech.
- Feeling sick.
- Changes in their vision.
- The person should wake up within 20 seconds.

Treatment:

- If still conscious lay them on their back and raise their legs, this should increase their blood pressure.
- If they can't lay down get them to sit with their head lowered between their knees.
- Taking beep breaths may help.
- If unconscious, check Airway and Breathing, if breathing maintain their airway and keep them on their back with legs raised if possible.
- If struggling to maintain airway place in recovery position.
- Ring 999/112 if you cannot wake them up after 1 minute, they have severely hurt themselves or are shaking or jerking from a seizure or fit.
- If not breathing or unsure start resuscitation.

Recovery Positions (Also known as the Safe Airway Positions)

Standard Recovery Position:

Place near arm out of the way, straight out or bent like picture.

Bring far away hand across chest, lock fingers palm to palm and place hand on side of head.

Bring up the opposite leg with hand on knee and use as a lever to pull person towards you.

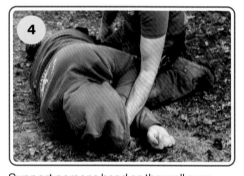

Support persons head as they roll over.

Bring knee up slightly to stop person moving onto their front.

Check airway is open and person is still breathing normally.

Single Spinal Recovery:

Place near arm hand first, palm up under the nape of the neck as shown, try not to move the head.

Keeping both legs straight, bring far away leg over near leg.

Bring far away arm across chest.

Place one hand on shoulder and other hand on waist, grab clothing if easier, pull person towards you.

Bring knee up slightly to stop person moving onto their front.

Check airway is open and person is still breathing normally.

Log Roll Multiple Rescuers:

Head end rescuer lie on ground and hold head securely with both hands.

Middle rescuer place near arm out of the way, straight out or bent like shown.

Middle rescuer bring far away arm across the chest.

Middle rescuer place one hand on shoulder and other hand on waist, grab clothing if easier.

Third rescuer place hand on waist grab clothing if easier grab the inside of the far away leg with other hand.

Head rescuer take charge, give command "Ready, Steady, Roll" work together to roll person unto their side. This is a good position for placing a blanket under a person and checking back for injuries.

Face Down to Face Up Single Rescuer:

1) Roll person towards the back of their head, place near arm in the position show "superman position".

2) Keeping legs straight, cross the further away leg over the near leg as shown.

3) Trap arm and grab the clothing at the top and bottom of spine as shown, straighten your back and roll person towards you.

4) Once on their back check airway and check breathing.

Baby Recovery Position:

Some books show babies being held face towards the rescuer. However we believe it is safer to have the baby facing away from you. This way you can monitor the breathing more easily and you are less likely to hold the baby too tightly.

Sickle Cell Disease

Sickle Cell Disease is the name given to a group of inherited conditions that affect the red blood cells by changing their shape from round to sickle shaped, which increases the risk of blood clots. This can also lead to possible Anaemia, a condition causing low haemoglobin in the red blood cells which transport oxygen around the body.

This lack of oxygen-rich blood can damage nerves and organs, including kidneys, liver and spleen, and can be fatal. The disease is particularly common in people with an African or Caribbean family background.

Signs and Symptoms:

- It has very few signs and symptoms and is normally found during blood testing.
- Very painful episodes especially in limbs.
- Headaches.
- Increased heart rate.
- Dizziness.
- Fainting.
- Can present as an infection like Parvovirus (Slapped Cheek Syndrome).

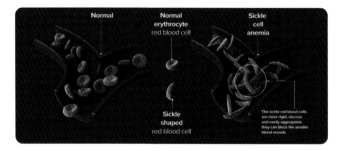

Treatment:

- Get them to drink plenty of fluids to avoid dehydration.
- Keep them warm.
- Avoid sudden temperature changes such as playing outdoors in the cold or entering cold water.
- Avoid strenuous exercise.
- Avoid alcohol or smoking.
- Avoid stress.
- Due to the risk of blood clotting leading to Heart Attack or Stroke if you have any concerns take to ED or call 999/112.

For more information, please go to www.sicklecellsociety.org

Anaphylaxis

Anaphylaxis is a severe and potentially life-threatening reaction to a trigger such as an allergen, causing the immune system, the body's natural defence system to overreact to this trigger, usually developing suddenly and getting worse very quickly.

Triggers:

- Foods – including nuts, milk, fish, shellfish, eggs and some fruits.
- Medicines – including some antibiotics and aspirin.
- Insect stings – particularly wasp and bee stings.
- Latex – a type of rubber found in some rubber gloves and condoms.

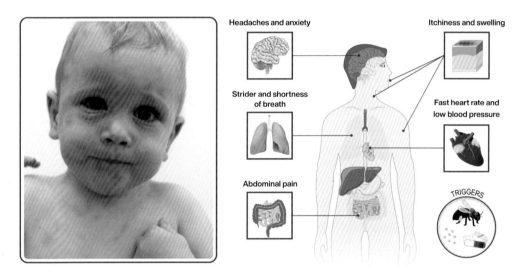

Signs and Symptoms:

- Feeling lightheaded or faint due to sudden drop in blood pressure.
- Swelling on the skin especially on the lips or face.
- Breathing difficulties – such as fast shallow breathing with possible wheezing.
- Raised heartrate and clammy skin.
- Cyanosis, look inside mouth and at tongue on darker skin.
- Confusion or anxiety.
- Sudden collapse with loss of consciousness.
- Other allergy signs and symptoms may include, itchy skin, raised rash (Hives), feeling sick or stomach pain.

Treatment:

- Lie the person down and raise their legs – if they are having breathing difficulties, they can be sat up but only for a very short time.

- Remove any trigger if possible – for example, carefully remove any stinger stuck in the skin.

- Use an adrenaline auto-injector without delay if the person has one, don't wait to see how bad it is. The auto-injector should be injected into the muscle in the patient's outer thigh. It can be given through clothes, however avoid pockets and seams.

- Call 999/112 for an ambulance immediately (even if they start to feel better) – mention that you think the person has anaphylaxis.

- If second auto-injector is available use after 5 minutes if the symptoms do not improve, inject in opposite leg, you can legally use another person's auto-injector if available.

- There are various auto-injectors on the market, make yourself aware of how to use any a person in your care might have.

- Be prepared to start resuscitation if required.

Stretch and flatten clothing on the upper thigh, turn out pocket, bare skin is best

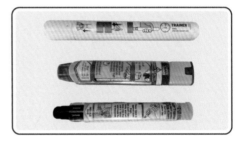

Jext-Pen Epi-Pen Emerade-Pen

Split upper thigh into 4 sections, inject in centre of top outer section

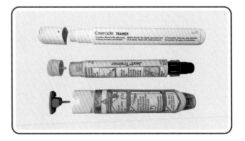

Pens with safety caps removed

Since Oct 2017 the Human Medicines Regulations allows schools to purchase adrenaline auto-injectors for emergency purposes, for more information please go to: www.anaphylaxis.org.uk and Https://assets.publishing.service.gov.uk/media/5a829e3940f0b6230269bcf4/Adrenaline_auto_injectors_in_schools.pdf

Asthma

Asthma is a common lung condition that causes breathing difficulties when the muscle wall surrounding the bronchial tubes in the lungs contracts and the lining of the airways becomes swollen and inflamed. These changes cause a narrowing of the airways which is further aggravated by an increase in secretions from the mucus membrane, which may actually block the smaller airways.

Causes and Triggers:

- Allergies (for example to house dust mites, animal fur or pollen).
- Smoke and pollution.
- Exercise especially in cold air.
- Infections like colds or flu.

Pathology of Asthma:

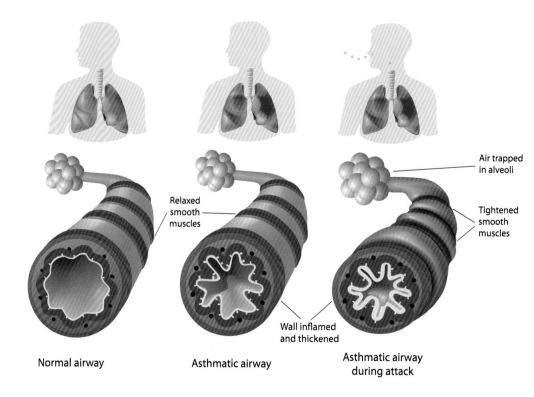

Relaxed smooth muscles

Air trapped in alveoli

Tightened smooth muscles

Wall inflamed and thickened

Normal airway

Asthmatic airway

Asthmatic airway during attack

Signs and Symptoms:

- Shortness of breath with an increased rate.
- Tightness in the chest, which may feel like a band is tightening around it.
- Coughing.
- Unable to talk in full sentences.
- Abdomen sucking inwards or chest being sucked in.
- Cyanosis grey/blue lips and skin, look inside mouth and at tongue on darker skin.
- Pallor (Unhealthy pale appearance) much harder to see on dark skin.
- A whistling sound especially when breathing out (wheezing).
- Fatigue.

Treatment:

- Sit person down and get them to sit up straight – try to keep them calm.
- Make them take one puff of their reliever inhaler (usually blue) every 30 to 60 seconds up to 10 puffs.
- A spacer should be used especially for children to ensure the medication reaches the lungs.
- If they feel worse or do not feel better after 10 puffs, call 999/112 for an ambulance.
- If the ambulance has not arrived after 10 minutes and their symptoms are not improving, repeat the above as required.
- If the person becomes unconscious, check Airway and Breathing, if breathing place in recovery position.
- If not breathing or unsure start resuscitation.

Since Oct 2014 the Human Medicines Regulations allows schools to purchase a salbutamol inhaler for emergency purposes, for more information please go to: www.asthma.org.uk and https://assets.publishing.service.gov.uk/media/5a74eb55ed915d3c7d528f98/emergency_inhalers_in_schools.pdf

Hyperventilation (Panic Attack)

Hyperventilation syndrome causes over-breathing when the body does not need it. It may be chronic, it is associated with symptoms felt in the body which may be very frightening and unpleasant but are not harmful.

It is very common, especially in females, those aged 15-55 and asthmatics and can happen after strong emotion such as anger, fear or excitement.

Signs and Symptoms:

- Shortness of breath, and a feeling of being unable to breathe.
- Tightness in the chest.
- Fear of dying.
- Tingling or numbness in both arms, fingers, toes or around the mouth.
- Dizziness, weakness, palpitations (fast heart beat).
- Flushed red and sweaty appearance, harder to see on dark skin, check their tongue.
- Feeling hot or cold.
- These can lead to a vicious cycle of feeling very ill, producing more anxiety and worsening of symptoms.

Treatment:

- Sit the person down.
- Get them to concentrate on slow regular breathing – in and out – aim for 8-10 breaths a minute.
- Get them to try a re-breathing technique by making a mask with their hands and placing them over their nose and mouth. Ask them to breathe in through their nose and out through their mouth.
- Sipping a glass of water can help.
- The use of a paper bag is no longer recommended by the NHS.
- Reassure the person that symptoms are not harmful and they do not have a serious medical problem.
- As their breathing slows, their symptoms should settle.
- If no improvement or getting worse ring 999/112 for assistance.

Breath-holding in Babies and Children

Breath-holding is when a baby or child stops breathing for up to 1 minute and may faint. It can happen when a child is frightened, upset, angry, or has a sudden shock or pain.

Although breath-holding can be scary for parents, with no specific treatment it's usually harmless and should eventually stop as children normally grow out of it by the age of 4 or 5. Children are not doing it on purpose and cannot control what happens when they have a breath-holding episode.

Signs and Symptoms:

- Child may cry and then be silent while holding their breath.
- Open their mouth as if going to cry but make no sound.
- Cyanosis grey/blue lips and skin, look inside mouth and at tongue on darker skin.
- Be floppy or stiff, or their body may jerk.
- Faint for 1 or 2 minutes.
- Your child may be sleepy or confused for a while afterwards.

Treatment:

Do

- Stay calm – it should pass in less than 1 minute.
- Lie the child on their side – do not pick them up.
- Gently blow air on their face.
- Stay with them until the episode ends.
- Make sure they cannot hit their head, arms or legs on anything.
- Reassure them and ensure they get plenty of rest afterwards.

Don't

- Do not shake your child or splash them with water.
- Do not put anything in their mouth (including your fingers).
- Do not give them mouth-to-mouth or CPR.
- Do not tell them off (they're not doing it deliberately).

Croup

Croup is a common viral condition that mainly affects babies' and young childrens' airways. It's usually mild, but it's important to consider getting help if you think your child has croup as they may need treatment.

Croup symptoms usually come on after a few days and are often worse at night.

Signs and Symptoms:

- A barking cough that sounds like a seal (you can search online to hear examples).
- A hoarse voice.
- Difficulty breathing.
- A rasping sound when breathing in.
- They may have had cold-like symptoms to begin with, such as a temperature, runny nose and cough.

Ring 999/112 if child has any of the following:

- Your child is struggling to breathe, watch for their abdomen sucking inwards or chest being sucked in.
- Cyanosis grey/blue lips and skin, look inside mouth and at tongue on darker skin.
- Unusually quiet and still.
- Their temperature is very high and they appear to be becoming worse.

Treatment:

- Croup usually gets better on its own within 48 hours.
- Sit the child up, try raising pillows in bed.
- Comfort them as crying can make it worse.
- Give plenty of fluids.
- Monitor temperature.
- Consider Paracetamol to ease a high temperature.
- Do not put child in a steamy room or inhale steam.
- Do not give cough or cold medication.

For more information, please go to www.nhs.uk/conditions/croup

Epiglottitis

Epiglottitis is inflammation and swelling of the epiglottis, caused by an infection or as a result of a throat injury. The epiglottis is a flap of tissue that sits beneath the tongue at the back of the throat. Its main function is to close over the windpipe (trachea) while you're eating to prevent food entering your airway.

Signs and Symptoms:

- The symptoms of epiglottitis usually develop quickly and get rapidly worse, although they can develop over a few days in older children and adults.
- Severe sore throat.
- Difficulty and pain when swallowing (Very common in adults).
- Difficulty breathing, which may improve when leaning forwards.
- Breathing that sounds abnormal and high-pitched (stridor).
- High temperature.
- Cyanosis grey/blue lips and skin, look inside mouth and at tongue on darker skin.
- Irritability and restlessness.
- Muffled or hoarse voice.
- Drooling (Very common in adults).

Treatment:

- Epiglottitis is a medical emergency, which can restrict the oxygen supply to the lungs.
- Keep them calm and try not to cause panic or distress.
- Sit the person up.
- Comfort them as crying can make it worse.
- Call 999/112 for an ambulance if you think the person has epiglottitis.
- While waiting for an ambulance, you should not attempt to examine their throat, place anything inside their mouth, or lay them on their back. This may make their symptoms worse .
- If the person becomes unconscious, check Airway and Breathing, if breathing place in recovery position.
- If not breathing or unsure start resuscitation.

For more information, please go to www.nhs.uk/conditions/epiglottitis

Heart Attack

A heart attack (Myocardial Infarction or MI) is a serious medical emergency in which the supply of blood to the heart is suddenly blocked, usually by a blood clot. A lack of blood to the heart may seriously damage the heart muscle and can be life threatening leading to a **Cardiac Arrest**.

Coronary heart disease (CHD) is the leading cause of heart attacks, a condition in which the major blood vessels that supply the heart get clogged by a blood clot caused by deposits of cholesterol, known as plaques.

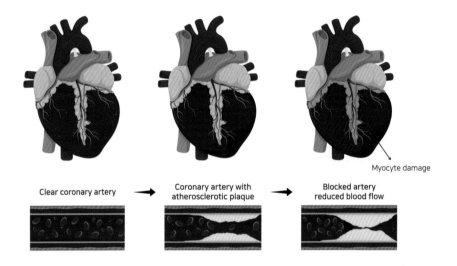

Myocyte damage

Clear coronary artery → Coronary artery with atherosclerotic plaque → Blocked artery reduced blood flow

Signs and Symptoms:

- Pale clammy skin, harder to see on dark skin check their tongue.
- Blue tinges to the skin and lips (cyanosis) look inside mouth and at tongue on darker skin.
- Chest pain – a feeling of pressure, heaviness, tightness or squeezing across their chest, however some people may only experience minor pain, similar to indigestion.
- Pain in other parts of the body – it can feel as if the pain is spreading from your chest to your arms (usually the left arm, but it can affect both arms), jaw, neck, back and abdomen.
- Feeling lightheaded or dizzy.
- Sweating.
- Shortness of breath.
- Feeling sick (Nausea) or being sick (Vomiting).
- An overwhelming feeling of anxiety (similar to a panic attack).
- While the most common symptom in both men and women is chest pain, women are more likely to have other symptoms such as shortness of breath, feeling or being sick and back or jaw pain.

Treatment:

- Call 999/122 immediately if you think someone might be having a heart attack, the faster you act, the better their chances.
- Ask for the nearest AED (Automatic External Defibrillator).
- Sit the person down, but keep upright, best on floor and bring knees up to chest.
- Reassure the person.
- Loosen tight clothing around the collar.
- If the person is over 16 years old consider asking them to chew a 300mg Dispersible Aspirin unless they have an allergy to Aspirin.
- If unconscious, check Airway and Breathing, if breathing place in recovery position.
- If not breathing or unsure Ring 999/112 back and start resuscitation.

Sit person down, bring their knees up to their chest and let them take their own GTN medication if they have any.

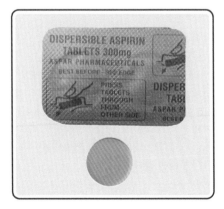 

Consider getting them to chew a 300mg Dispersible Aspirin if over 16 years old and not allergic.

Get an AED on standby in case they go in to cardiac arrest, just don't fit until required.

Angina

Angina is chest pain caused by reduced blood flow to the heart muscles normally caused by a build up of cholesterol, known as plaques (atherosclerosis). It's not usually life threatening, but it's a warning sign that you could be at risk of a **Heart Attack** or **Stroke**.

Signs and Symptoms:

- History of Angina.
- The main symptom of angina is chest pain.
- Chest feels tight, dull or heavy – it may spread to your arms, neck, jaw or back.
- Pale clammy skin, harder to see on dark skin check their tongue.
- Is normally triggered by physical exertion or stress.
- Feeling sick or breathless.
- Should stop within a few minutes of resting.

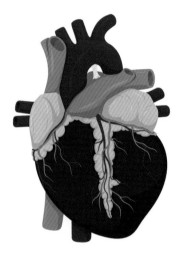

Coronary artery with atherosclerotic plaque

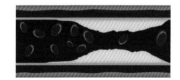

Treatment:

- Sit the person down, but keep upright, best on floor and bring knees up to chest.
- Reassure the person.
- Loosen tight clothing around the collar.
- They may have medication called GTN, this is a spray which they should take under their tongue. Make sure they are sitting down before they take the spray as it will drop their blood pressure and may cause them to pass out.
- If they don't feel better within a few minutes of resting Call 999/122 as they could be having a heart attack so the faster you act, the better their chances.
- Ask for the nearest AED (Automatic External Defibrillator).
- If unconscious, check Airway and Breathing, if breathing place in recovery position.
- If not breathing or unsure Ring 999/112 back and start resuscitation.

Cardiac Arrest

Cardiac arrest is when the heart suddenly and unexpectedly stops pumping, thus reducing blood flow to the brain and other vital organs and is most commonly caused by an irregular heart rhythm called **Ventricular Fibrillation (VF)**. This rapid, erratic rhythm prevents the heart from pumping blood correctly. It can be brought on by the following conditions:

- Heart muscle disease (Cardiomyopathie).
- Heart valve disease.
- Inflammation of the heart muscle (Myocarditis).
- Heart attack.
- Severe haemorrhage.
- Hypoxia.
- Electrocution.
- Drug overdose.

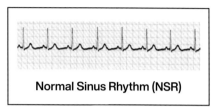

Normal Sinus Rhythm (NSR)

AED will advise no shock start CPR if required.

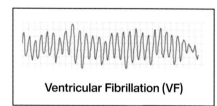

Ventricular Fibrillation (VF)

AED will advise "Shock".

Signs and Symptoms:

- Sudden loss of consciousness.
- Lack of pulse.
- Not breathing normally (Noisy or Agonal Gasping).

Treatment:

- Call 999/122 immediately if you think someone might be having a cardiac arrest. The faster you act, the better their chances.
- Ask for the nearest AED (Automatic External Defibrillator).
- Start resuscitation (CPR) (See pages 19-21) depending on age.
- Use AED as soon as it arrives (See pages 22-23).

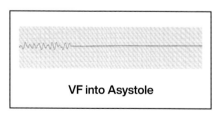

VF into Asystole

AED shock should change rhythm from VF to Asystole.

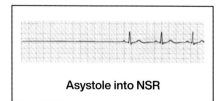

Asystole into NSR

Hearts own pacemaker should restart heart from Asystole into NSR.

For more information, please go to www.bhf.org.uk

Stroke

There are 2 main types of stroke: **Ischaemic** and **Haemorrhagic**.

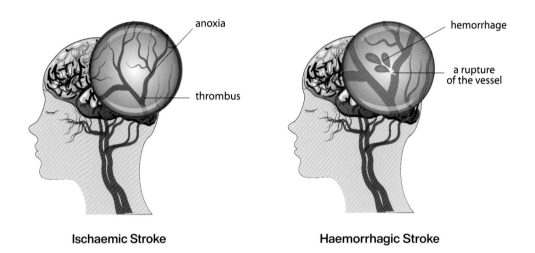

anoxia

thrombus

hemorrhage

a rupture of the vessel

Ischaemic Stroke

Haemorrhagic Stroke

Ischaemic Strokes are the most common type of stroke, caused when a blood clot (Thrombus) completely blocks the flow of blood and oxygen to the brain causing Anoxia. These blood clots typically form in areas where the arteries have been narrowed or blocked over time by fatty deposits (plaques).

Another possible cause of ischaemic stroke is a type of irregular heartbeat called Atrial Fibrillation (AF), caused when blood clots in the heart that break apart and end up in the blood vessels that supply the brain.

Haemorrhagic Strokes are less common than ischaemic strokes. They happen when a blood vessel inside the skull bursts and bleeds into and around the brain.

The main cause of haemorrhagic stroke is high blood pressure, which can weaken the arteries in the brain and make them more likely to split or rupture.

TIA (Transient Ischaemic Attack) Symptoms of a stroke that disappear quickly and in less than 24 hours may mean they had a Transient Ischaemic Attack (TIA) also known as a mini-stroke.

Even if the symptoms disappear while you're waiting for the ambulance, it's still important to go to hospital for an assessment.

Signs and Symptoms:

As different parts of our brain control different parts of our body, their signs and symptoms will depend on the part of their brain affected and the extent of the damage.

The main stroke signs can be remembered with the word **BEFAST**:

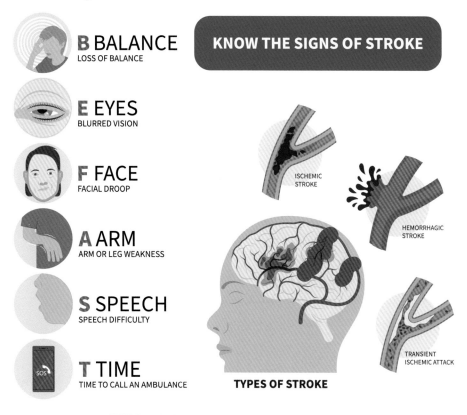

B BALANCE
LOSS OF BALANCE

KNOW THE SIGNS OF STROKE

E EYES
BLURRED VISION

F FACE
FACIAL DROOP

A ARM
ARM OR LEG WEAKNESS

S SPEECH
SPEECH DIFFICULTY

T TIME
TIME TO CALL AN AMBULANCE

ISCHEMIC STROKE

HEMORRHAGIC STROKE

TRANSIENT ISCHEMIC ATTACK

TYPES OF STROKE

Unequal pupils could be a sign of a Stroke

Treatment:

- Call 999/112 immediately and ask for an ambulance.
- Keep the person as still as possible, sitting up is ok.
- Reassure.
- If unconscious, check Airway and Breathing, if breathing place in recovery position.
- If not breathing or unsure Ring 999/112 back and start resuscitation.

For more information, please go to www.stroke.org.uk

Seizures, Fits and Convulsions

Seizures, Fits and Convulsions can affect people in different ways, depending on which part of the brain is involved. Many cause bursts of electrical activity in the brain that temporarily affect how it works. There are many causes including Epilepsy, Trauma, Hypoxia, High Temperature and Drugs.

Signs and Symptoms of Epilepsy:

Epileptic seizures can have two phases classed as a tonic-clonic seizure.

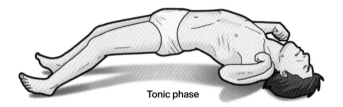

Tonic phase

During the "Tonic" phase:

- They lose consciousness and will not be aware of what is happening.
- Their muscles go stiff and if standing will collapse.
- They may cry out as air is pushed up through their voice box.
- They may clench their teeth and bite their tongue or lips.

Clonic phase

During the "Clonic" phase:

- Their limbs jerk quickly and rhythmically.
- They may lose control of their bladder and bowels.
- Their teeth may remain clenched affecting their breathing causing slight hypoxia around the mouth, harder to see on dark skin.
- They may have sick or blood-stained saliva in their mouth if they have bitten their lips or tongue.

Other Signs and Symptoms:

- They may start losing awareness and just start staring blankly into space.
- Complain of strange sensation such as a rising in the stomach, unusual smells or tastes, or a tingling feeling in their arms and legs.
- History of being ill with a temperature.
- They may become stiff and their arms and legs may begin to twitch.
- They will lose consciousness and may wet or soil themselves.
- Cyanosis grey/blue lips and skin, harder to see on dark skin.
- Their eyes may roll back.

Treatment:

- Check for Danger to you and the person, only move the person if they are in imminent danger.
- Check response then airway, they may have clenched their teeth and bitten through their tongue, if their mouth is full of blood you need to put them in the recovery position.
- Check for breathing, as their airway may be slightly obstructed you should hear them sucking air through their nose and teeth.
- Time the seizure if possible.
- Support their head and limbs as required to stop them injuring themselves during the fitting stage.
- Loosen tight clothing around their neck to aid breathing.
- Remove any bedding and extra clothing to help with temperature reduction.
- Open window and provide fan if environment is hot.
- When seizure stops, check Airway and Breathing, if breathing place in recover position.
- It can take a while for the person to recover so stay with them and talk to them calmly until they recover.
- Don't use wet flannels to cool children and babes as this may over cool them, leading to a raising of the core temp.
- Person may have emergency medication to be used after 5 minutes of continual fitting.

Call 999/112 and ask for an ambulance if:

- It is the first time they have had a seizure.
- The seizure lasts longer than is usual for them.
- The seizure lasts more than 5 minutes, if you do not know how long their seizures usually last.
- The person does not regain full consciousness, or has several seizures without regaining consciousness.
- The person is seriously injured during the seizure.
- You suspect the seizure is being caused by another serious illness – for example, meningitis.
- They are having breathing difficulties.
- If not breathing or unsure Ring 999/112 back and start resuscitation.

Febrile Seizures (Febrile Convulsions)

- Febrile Seizures (febrile convulsions) are fits that can happen when a child has a fever. They most often happen between the ages of 6 months and 3 years.
- The cause of febrile seizures is unknown, although in most cases they are caused by high temperature from an infection.
- There may also be a genetic link to febrile seizures, as the chances of having a seizure are increased if a close family member has a history of them.
- However, these seizures are usually harmless and last less than 5 minutes and almost all children make a complete recovery afterwards.

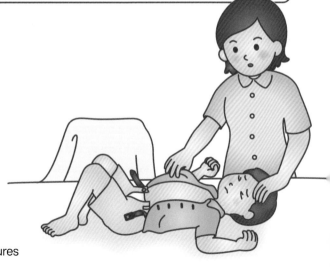

For more information please go to:
www.epilepsy.org.uk
www.epilepsyresearch.org.uk
www.nhs.uk/conditions/febrile-seizures

Diabetes

There are two types of Diabetes, **Type 1** and **Type 2**

Type 2 Diabetes is becoming a very common condition caused by problems with the hormone insulin not working effectively which in turn can cause the level of sugar (glucose) in the blood to become too high.

It can become a life long condition which can cause serious problems with the eyes, heart and nerves, often linked to being overweight or inactive, or having a family history of Type 2 Diabetes.

It rarely needs first aid treatment, more likely to bring on conditions like heart attack or stroke.

Type 1 Diabetes happens when your body cannot produce enough of a hormone called insulin. The body needs insulin to help most of the cells in your body use the sugar (glucose) to carry out their functions. However brain cells can take sugar (glucose) straight from your blood without the need for insulin.

Therefore it is very important that the condition is identified in people quickly so the correct treatment can be provided. It is more common for babies and children to be missed, so we should look out for the following **Four Ts**.

Toilet – A baby might have heavier nappies, or a child who is usually dry at night might start wetting the bed.

Thirsty – A child may ask for a drink more often, finish drinks very quickly or you may notice they generally drink more.

Tired – A child's teacher may let you know they're having trouble staying awake in school, or a baby might start napping more or for longer.

Thinner – A child may feel or look thinner when you're getting them dressed or their clothes may feel looser.

Once the condition has been identified it can be controlled through the person taking external source of insulin and keeping a close watch on their sugar (glucose) levels through close watch on their diet.

From a first aid point of view we just need to identify low **(Hypoglycaemia)** or high **(Hyperglycaemia)** blood glucose, low being more dangerous in the short term than high.

Hypoglycaemia (Low)

Signs and Symptoms:

- Pale clammy skin, harder to see on dark skin check their tongue.
- Sweating.
- Being anxious or irritable.
- Feeling hungry.
- Confusion.
- Difficulty concentrating.
- Blurred vision.
- Trembling and feeling shaky.
- Unconsciousness.

| Sweating | Pallor | Irritability | Hunger | Lack of Co-ordination | Sleepiness |

Treatment:

- If conscious get them to eat around 15 grams of fast acting carbohydrate, from sugary drinks, fruit juice, glucose or dextrose tables, 4 large jelly babies or 2 tubes of rescue gel.
- Repeat after 15 mins if no improvement.
- Sugary foods containing fat like chocolate or cake don't work so well.
- You need to be careful as too much sugar could cause Hyperglycaemia.
- If they response get them to eat a longer lasting carbohydrate like biscuits, sandwich or meal.
- If unconscious, check airway and breathing, if breathing place in recovery position and ring 999/112, it is not recommended you place anything in their mouth as the chance of choking might be high.
- If not breathing or unsure Ring 999/112 back and start resuscitation.

Rescue Gel

Hyperglycaemia (High)

Signs and Symptoms:

- Feeling very thirsty.
- Feeling very tired all the time.
- Having fruity-smelling breath.
- Blurred vision.
- Semi-conscious and struggling to stay awake.

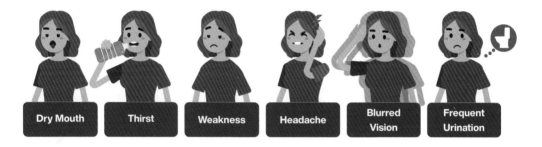

| Dry Mouth | Thirst | Weakness | Headache | Blurred Vision | Frequent Urination |

Treatment:

- Very high blood sugar levels can lead to a serious problem called Diabetic Ketoacidosis. (DKA) when the body starts to break down fat in the liver for energy when there is not enough insulin to allow enough glucose into cells, so the body switches to burning fat which leads to a build up of acid (ketones) in the blood.
- This can be life threatening and should be treated in hospital.
- DKA can develop over a few hours. Things like infections and drinking too much alcohol are common triggers for DKA.
- If unconscious, check airway and breathing, if breathing place in recovery position and ring 999/112, it is not recommended you place anything in their mouth as the chance of choking might be high.
- If not breathing or unsure Ring 999/112 back and start resuscitation.

Most Type 1 Diabetics will have some means of checking their blood glucose levels, a simple machine or an app on their phone connected to their body. If you know the diabetic ask them to show you how to check their blood glucose just in case you ever need to.

Meningitis

Meningitis is an infection of the protective membranes that surround the brain and spinal cord (meninges). It is usually caused by a bacterial or viral infection. Bacterial meningitis is rarer but more serious than viral meningitis. Infections that cause meningitis can be spread through:

- Sneezing.
- Coughing.
- Kissing.

Meningitis is usually caught from people who carry these viruses or bacteria in their nose or throat but are not ill themselves.

It can affect anyone, but is most common in babies, young children, teenagers and young adults. Meningitis can be very serious if not treated quickly. It can cause life-threatening blood poisoning (SEPSIS see page 62) and result in permanent damage to the brain or nerves.

Reasons

bacteria   viruses   fungal

50% death without treatment

Signs and Symptoms:

They can develop suddenly in any order and may include:

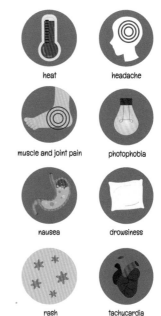

heat   headache

muscle and joint pain   photophobia

nausea   drowsiness

rash   tachycardia

- A high temperature (fever).
- Being sick.
- A headache.
- A rash that does not fade when a glass is rolled over it (but a rash will not always develop). For darker skin check inside of mouth, palms of hands and souls of feet.
- A stiff neck.
- A dislike of bright lights (Photophobia).
- Drowsiness or unresponsiveness.
- Seizures (fits).

Treatment:

- Call 999/112 for an ambulance or go to your nearest ED immediately if you think you or someone you look after could have meningitis or sepsis.
- Trust your instincts and do not wait for all the symptoms to appear or until a rash develops. Someone with meningitis or sepsis can get a lot worse very quickly.
- Reassure.
- If unconscious, check Airway and Breathing, if breathing place in recovery position.
- If not breathing or unsure Ring 999/112 back and start resuscitation.
- People with suspected meningitis will usually have tests in hospital to confirm the diagnosis and check whether the condition is the result of a viral or bacterial infection.
- Bacterial meningitis usually needs to be treated in hospital for at least a week.
- Viral meningitis tends to get better on its own within 7 to 10 days and can often be treated at home.
- Most people with bacterial meningitis who are treated quickly will also make a full recovery, although some are left with serious long-term problems. Overall, it's estimated up to 1 in every 10 cases of bacterial meningitis is fatal.

For more information go to: www.meningitis.org/meningitis/check-symptoms

Sepsis

Sepsis is a life threatening reaction to an infection when the immune system overreacts to the infection and starts to damage the body's own tissues and organs. You cannot catch sepsis from another person. It is sometimes called septicaemia or blood poisoning.

Sepsis can be especially hard to spot in:

- Babies and young children.
- People with dementia.
- People with a learning disability.
- People who have difficulty communicating.

Some of the sources of possible infection:

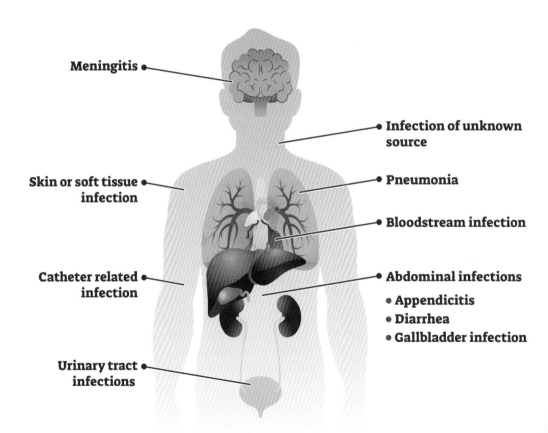

Meningitis

Infection of unknown source

Skin or soft tissue infection

Pneumonia

Bloodstream infection

Catheter related infection

Abdominal infections
- Appendicitis
- Diarrhea
- Gallbladder infection

Urinary tract infections

Signs and Symptoms in Babies and Children:

- Blue, pale or blotchy skin, lips or tongue – on brown or black skin, blueness may be easier to see on the lips, tongue or gums, under the nails or around the eyes.
- A rash that does not fade when you roll a glass over it, the same as meningitis.
- Difficulty breathing, you may notice grunting noises or their stomach sucking under their ribcage, breathlessness or breathing very fast.
- A weak high pitched cry that's not like their normal cry.
- Not responding like they normally do, or not interested in feeding or normal activities.
- Being sleepier than normal or difficult to wake.
- Raised temperature.
- Has not had a wee all day or in the last 12 hours or a dry nappy.
- Keeps vomiting and cannot keep food or milk down.

Extra Signs and Symptoms in Adults and Older Children:

- Acting confused, slurred speech or not making sense.
- Feels very unwell or like there's something seriously wrong.
- Blue, pale or blotchy skin, lips or tongue – on brown or black skin, blueness may be easier to see on the lips, tongue or gums, under the nails or around the eyes.
- A rash that does not fade when you roll a glass over it, the same as meningitis.
- Difficulty breathing, breathlessness or breathing very fast.
- Very high temperature, feels hot or cold to the touch, or is shivering.
- Has swelling, pain, redness, itchiness, pus or feels hot around a cut or wound.
- They can be like symptoms of other conditions, including flu or a chest infection.

Treatment:

- Sepsis is life threatening and can be hard to spot so if you think someone has signs and symptoms of sepsis, trust your instincts, call 999/112 or go to ED.
- Lying down might be the best position, however if they are having breathing difficulties they can be sat up.
- Reassure.
- If unconscious, check Airway and Breathing, if breathing place in recovery position.
- If not breathing or unsure Ring 999/112 back and start resuscitation.

For more information go to: www.sepsistrust.org/about/about-sepsis

Identifyling Heat Conditions with a Thermometer

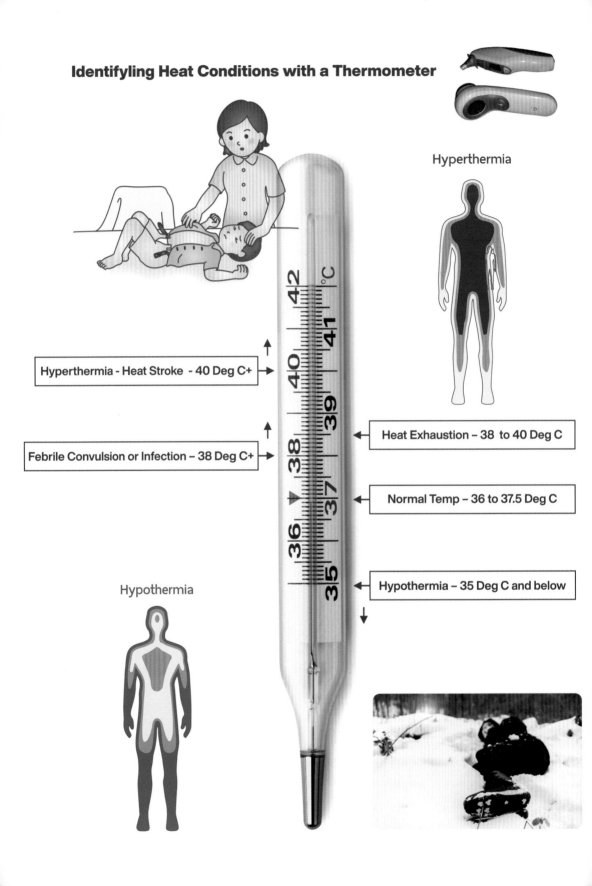

Hyperthermia

Hyperthermia - Heat Stroke - 40 Deg C+

Febrile Convulsion or Infection – 38 Deg C+

Heat Exhaustion – 38 to 40 Deg C

Normal Temp – 36 to 37.5 Deg C

Hypothermia

Hypothermia – 35 Deg C and below

Frost Bite

Frostbite is damage to the skin and tissue caused by exposure to freezing temperatures and can affect any part of your body, but the extremities, such as the hands, feet, ears, nose and lips, are most likely to be affected.

Signs and Symptoms:

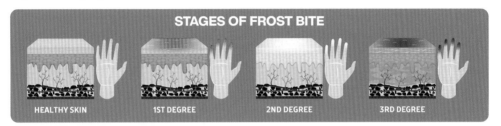

Treatment:

Cold Water Shock and Drowning

As it can take up to 30 minutes even in really cold water to succumb to dying of hypothermia, there is more chance that unless they have a way of surviving past the point of cold water shock and swim failure (like wearing a lifejacket), they will probably drown before becoming hypothermic.

The term **'cold water shock'** refers to the reactions a body takes to protect itself when entering cold water There are three stages that a body goes through during cold water shock. They will gasp for breath, followed by rapid breathing (hyperventilation) which quickly gets out of control , their blood pressure shoots up as the body tries to keep the blood warm by moving it towards the middle of the body (this is why people go pale when they are cold). This sudden rise in blood pressure can be fatal for people with a pre-existing heart condition. Each year a number of people who are suspected of drowning, turn out to have had a cardiac arrest.

As the body's muscles cool, the strength, endurance and muscle control reduces to the point when they can't swim any longer (called **'swim failure'**). If they have not got out of the water or managed to get hold of something they will most probably drown.

Drowning

The events that result in Drowning:

- Struggling to keep the airway clear of water due to swim failure.
- Initial submersion and breath-holding.
- Aspiration of water.
- Unconsciousness.
- Cardio-respiratory arrest.

Rescue and Treatment for Drowning:

- They need to be rescued from the water as soon as possible.
- If still in the water and conscious ask then to lie on their back with their arms and legs outstretched and head back, this should help them float.
- Throw before you go, anything that floats or a rope.
- Call 999/112 ask for Coastguard if near the Sea and Fire Service if inland.
- Only enter the water as a last resort if you feel confident, take a float or rope, wade in slowly to avoid cold shock and watch your footing.
- Consider Hypothermia when rescuing and try and keep them horizontal.
- If unconscious, check Airway and Breathing which will be hard to detect, so check for longer, if breathing treat for Hypothermia and consider the recovery position.
- If not breathing or unsure start resuscitation for drowning, 5 rescue breaths followed by chest compressions for up to one minute before going for help if on your own.

Secondary Drowning

Secondary drowning is used to describe a delayed-onset of breathing problems in someone who seems to be recovering after a submersion event which can be caused by the complications that occur as a result of aspiration of any foreign substances, including fresh/salt/chlorinated water or vomit into the lungs.

This in turn can cause progressive injury and inflammation within the lungs, as the lungs become more ineffective and fluid accumulates within the lungs their condition will deteriorate.

Signs and Symptoms:

- Coughing.
- Increased respiratory rate and work of breathing.
- Low oxygen levels with hypoxia.
- Altered mental status (irritability or lethargy).
- Unconsciousness.
- Failure of breathing.

Treatment:

- A close eye should be kept on someone who seems to be recovering after a submersion event, especially if it was unexpected.
- Sit the person down, but keep upright, best on floor and bring knees up to chest.
- If they start to show any of the signs and symptoms take to ED or call 999/112.
- If unconscious, check Airway and Breathing which might be hard to detect, if breathing consider the recovery position.
- If not breathing or unsure start resuscitation for drowning, 5 rescue breaths followed by chest compression for up to one minute before going for help if on your own.

Hypothermia

Hypothermia is a dangerous condition which occurs when the body starts losing heat quicker than it can maintain it, dropping the body temperature below 35C (normal body temperature is around 37C). It's a medical emergency that needs to be treated in hospital.

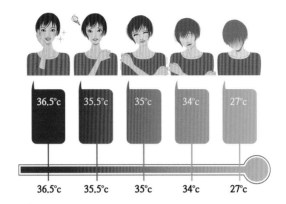

| 36.5°c | 35.5°c | 35°c | 34°c | 27°c |

Signs and Symptoms:

- Pale, cold and clammy skin, harder to see on dark skin check their tongue.
- Trembling and feeling shaky.
- Shivering to try and warm the body.
- Shivering will stop if not treated as body tries to reserve glucose.
- Being anxious or irritable.
- Fatigue.
- Problems speaking.
- Confusion with hand eye coordination problems.
- Rapid breathing become shallow if not treated.
- Rapid pulse becoming weak if not treated.
- Difficulty concentrating with dizziness with blurred vision.
- Unconscious.

Water Temp Deg C	Exhaustion – Unconsciousness	Expected Survival Time
10-16	1 to 2 Hours	1 to 6 Hours
4-10	30 to 60 Minutes	1 to 3 Hours
0-4	15 to 30 Minutes	30 to 90 Minutes
>0	Under 15 Minutes	0 to 45 Minutes

Average sea temperature in the British Isles ranges from **6-10 °C** in the winter to **15-20 °C** in the summer depending on region.

Average inland waters can be as low as **Zero** in winter to as high as the **Mid 20s** in peak summer.

Treatment:

- Call 999/112 as soon as possible.
- Moving people should be done with care, no sudden movements, keep as horizontal as possible due to low blood pressure, especially when removing from cold water as hydrostatic pressure will be lost and blood pressure can drop suddenly.
- Try and get them into shelter or build shelter round them and insulate from the ground.
- Once rescued laying them down with legs raised would be the best position.
- Remove any wet clothing, try and dry the skin, put them in dry clothing, wrap in a blanket, sleeping bag or dry towels, making sure their head is covered.
- Give them a warm non-alcoholic drink and some sugary food like chocolate if they're fully awake.
- Keep them awake by talking to them until help arrives and make sure you or someone else stays with them.
- Move to a warmer environment and let them passively rewarm to room temperature.
- For mild hypothermia a tepid bath or shower can be used with care, but they must sit or lie down and not be left alone.
- If unconscious, check Airway and Breathing which will be hard to detect, so check for longer, if breathing consider the recovery position.
- If not breathing or unsure Ring 999/112 back and start resuscitation.

The key thing is **NOT** to try and warm the person up too quickly as this can draw the warmest blood away from the core to the surface thus drawing colder blood into the core which can lead to **Cardiac Arrest**.

Things not to do:

- Do not use a hot bath, hot water bottle or heat lamp to warm them up.
- Do not rub their arms, legs, feet or hands.
- Do not give them alcohol to drink.
- Avoid wrapping Tin Foil Blankets over wet clothing or next to skin, as this prevents re-warming, they are ok for insulating from the ground or keeping rain off.
- Avoid person to person body warming as this can result in two casualties.

Heat Exhaustion

Heat exhaustion does not usually need emergency medical help if you can cool the person down within 30 minutes. If it turns into heatstroke, it needs to be treated as an emergency.

Signs and Symptoms:

- Tiredness.
- Dizziness.
- Headache.
- Feeling sick or being sick.
- Excessive sweating and skin becoming pale and clammy or getting a heat rash, this can be harder to see on dark skin.
- Cramps in the arms, legs and stomach.
- Fast breathing or heartbeat.
- Temperature can be normal or slightly raised.
- Very thirsty.
- Weakness.

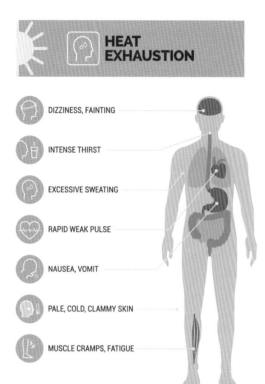

Treatment:

- Move them to a cool place.
- Sit the person down, but keep upright, best on floor and bring knees up to chest.
- Remove all unnecessary clothing like a jacket or socks.
- Get them to drink a sports or rehydration drink, or cool water.
- Stay with them until they're better.
- They should start to cool down and feel better within 30 minutes.

Heat Stroke

Signs and Symptoms:

- If heat exhaustion is not resolved within 30 minutes of resting in a cool place, being cooled and drinking fluids consider heatstroke.
- A very high temperature 40c and over.
- Hot skin that's not sweating and might look red, this can be harder to see on dark skin.
- In heatstroke brought on by hot weather, the skin will feel hot and dry to the touch. However, in heatstroke brought on by strenuous exercise, their skin may feel dry or slightly moist.
- A fast heartbeat.
- Fast breathing or shortness of breath.
- Confusion and lack of coordination.
- A seizure or fit.
- Loss of consciousness falling into a coma.
- Headache, their head may throb.

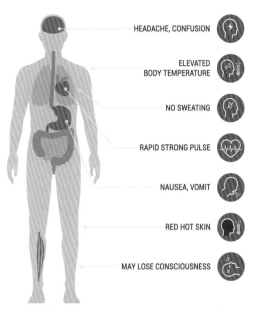

HEADACHE, CONFUSION

ELEVATED BODY TEMPERATURE

NO SWEATING

RAPID STRONG PULSE

NAUSEA, VOMIT

RED HOT SKIN

MAY LOSE CONSCIOUSNESS

FIRST AID

CALL EMERGENCY SERVICE

TAKE IMMEDIATE ACTION TO COOL THE PERSON

Treatment:

- Call 999/112 as this is a medical emergency.
- Sit the person down, but keep upright, best on floor and bring knees up to chest.
- Cool their skin – spray or sponge them with cool water and fan them.
- Get cold packs, wrapped in a cloth and put under the armpits or on the back of neck.
- Cover the person with cool damp sheets.
- If unconscious, check Airway and Breathing, if breathing place in recovery position.
- If not breathing or unsure Ring 999/112 back and start resuscitation.

Bleeding

If someone is bleeding, the main aim is to prevent further blood loss and minimise the effects of shock. Apply disposable gloves if possible and follow the Haemorrhage flow chart below.

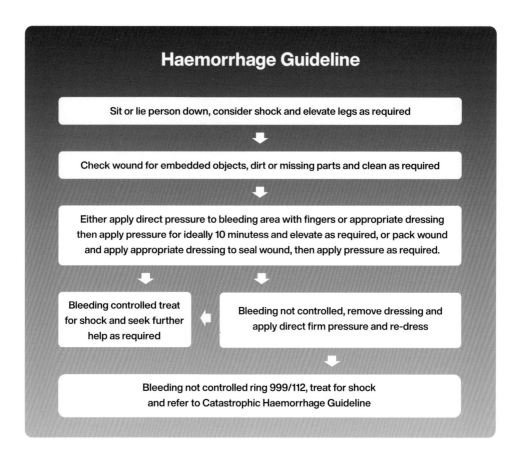

Haemorrhage Guideline

Sit or lie person down, consider shock and elevate legs as required

Check wound for embedded objects, dirt or missing parts and clean as required

Either apply direct pressure to bleeding area with fingers or appropriate dressing then apply pressure for ideally 10 minutess and elevate as required, or pack wound and apply appropriate dressing to seal wound, then apply pressure as required.

Bleeding controlled treat for shock and seek further help as required

Bleeding not controlled, remove dressing and apply direct firm pressure and re-dress

Bleeding not controlled ring 999/112, treat for shock and refer to Catastrophic Haemorrhage Guideline

Types of bleeding:

Arterial Bleeding - the most serious type of bleeding, oxygenated and bright red, shooting from the body with each heartbeat.

Venous Bleeding - less serious, dark red and trickling from the body.

Capillary Bleeding - least serious and most common, bright red, oozing from body.

Wound Cleaning

It's important if possible to clean a wound before applying a plaster or dressing, this will help reduce the risk of infection and encourage the healing process.

Follow these steps:

- Wash and dry your hands thoroughly if time allows.
- Wear disposable gloves and other PPE as required if available.
- Tell them what you're doing and make sure they're sitting or lying down.
- Don't try to remove anything embedded in the wound (See page 90-91).
- Rinse the wound under running tap water.
- Soak a gauze pad or cloth in saline solution or tap water, or use an alcohol-free wipe, and gently dab or wipe the skin with it – don't use antiseptic as this may damage the skin.
- Gently pat the area dry using a clean towel or gauze swab, but nothing fluffy such as a cotton wool ball as strands of material can get stuck to the wound.
- Apply a sterile dressing, such as a non-adhesive pad with a bandage, a plaster or a waterproof dressing if available.
- If blood soaks through the dressing (See page 72).

When to seek medical advice:

Visit your nearest Minor Injuries Unit (MIU), ED or call NHS 111 if the wound:

- Does not stop bleeding especially if taking any blood thinning medication.
- It is very large or very deep.
- Has dirt or something embedded in it.
- Is too painful for you to successfully clean.
- Is near to a major blood vessel or joint.
- Becomes red and swollen or has pus coming out – it may be infected.
- Was caused by a bite – all animal and human bites need medical attention.

Catastrophic Bleeding (Haemorrhage)

Catastrophic Haemorrhage is bleeding that is life threatening and if not quickly controlled could lead to death, which is why it has to be considered and dealt with at the start of the **PRIMARY SURVEY**. Follow the **Catastrophic Haemorrhage Guideline**.

Employers as part of their First Aid Risk Assessment should weigh up the chance of a Catastrophic Haemorrhage occurring in their workplace and then consider if the appropriate equipment should be provided. For instance, if chainsaws are used, then it would be reasonable to have equipment to deal with this sort of injury.

The minimum equipment required to deal with this type of injury would be the following.

Tourniquet

These have been designed for quick simple application to a Limb and can be used by an individual on their own. There are lots of different types on the market, best advice would be whatever one you purchase, read the instruction for use provided and hold an awareness session with all staff who may have to use it, following the Catastrophic Haemorrhage guideline opposite. This will ensure they are confident in its use.

Improvised tourniquet

Standard tourniquet

Tourniquet in use

Haemostatic Gauze Dressing

This type of dressing is impregnated with chemicals that work by encouraging some of the red blood cells to become sticky and form a clot which helps to seal wound and control the bleeding. Again, there are lots of different types on the market, best advice would be whatever one you purchase, read the instruction for use provided and hold an awareness session with all staff who may have to use it, following the Catastrophic Haemorrhage guideline opposite. This will ensure they are confident in its use.

Large Wound Dressing or Trauma Dressing

Standard First Aid Kit dressings may not be large enough to deal with a large wound. Again, there are lots of different types on the market, best advice would be whatever one you purchase, read the instruction for use provided and hold an awareness session with all staff who may have to use it, following the Catastrophic Haemorrhage guideline below. This will ensure they are confident in its use.

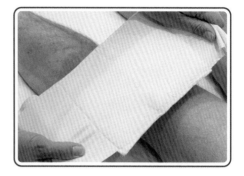

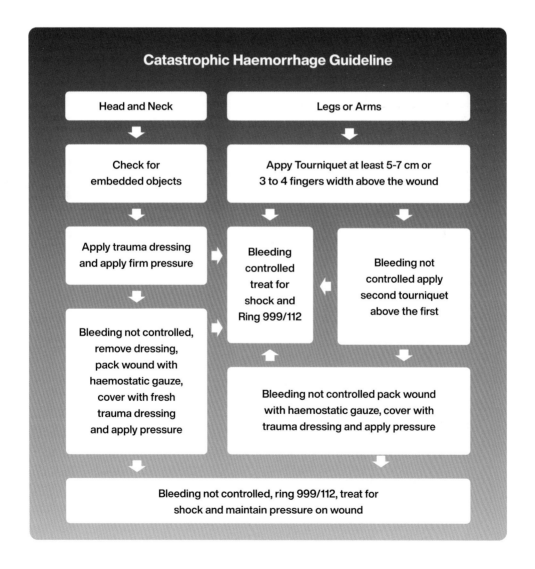

Catastrophic Haemorrhage Guideline

Head and Neck	Legs or Arms

Head and Neck
→ Check for embedded objects
→ Apply trauma dressing and apply firm pressure
→ Bleeding not controlled, remove dressing, pack wound with haemostatic gauze, cover with fresh trauma dressing and apply pressure

Legs or Arms
→ Appy Tourniquet at least 5-7 cm or 3 to 4 fingers width above the wound
→ Bleeding controlled treat for shock and Ring 999/112
→ Bleeding not controlled apply second tourniquet above the first
→ Bleeding not controlled pack wound with haemostatic gauze, cover with trauma dressing and apply pressure

Bleeding not controlled, ring 999/112, treat for shock and maintain pressure on wound

Trauma - Head Injuries

Concussion is the sudden but short-lived loss of mental function that occurs after a blow or other injury to the head, it is the most common but least serious type of brain injury.

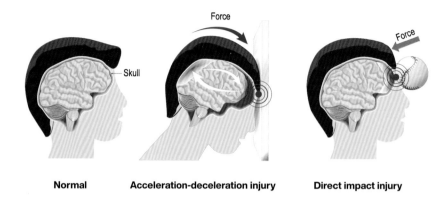

Normal **Acceleration-deceleration injury** **Direct impact injury**

Compression is normally caused by swelling or bleeding in the skull putting pressure on the brain, which can occur from injury, a ruptured blood vessel, a tumour or infection like meningitis.

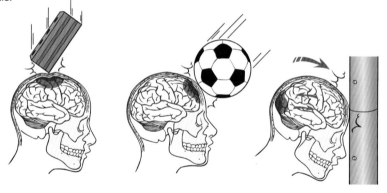

Fractured skull is when bone in the skull has been broken by an injury or trauma. As the skull is very strong, it takes a lot of force to damage it. This might be from falling from a height, a car accident or a direct blow to the head.

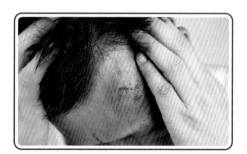
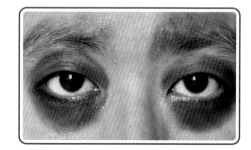

It is not always easy to identify the specific type of head injury just from the Signs and Symptoms, so the following is a general list of possible Signs and Symptoms.

- History of a recent head injury with apparent recovery but then a deterioration in level of consciousness (AVPU) (See page 11).
- Wound, lump, swelling or dent on the head.
- Bruising especially behind the ears or around the eyes.
- Headache or feeling pressure in their head.
- Confusion, disorientation, drowsiness or amnesia.
- Dizziness or balance problems.
- Nausea or vomiting.
- Clear or straw coloured fluid or blood coming from the nose or ears.
- Seizure or convulsion.
- Neck pain.
- Blurred vision, unequal or dilated pupils, sensitivity to light or noise.
- More emotional, sad, nervous or anxious.
- Irritability, restlessness, impulsivity and self-control problems.
- Or they just don't feel right.

Unequal

Dilated

Treatment:

- Don PPE as required.
- Conduct primary and secondary survey, treat any visible injuries and consider spinal injury.
- Consider applying a cold compress or cool pack to effected area for short periods to help reduce or prevent any swelling.
- Rest and avoid stress consider treating for shock.
- If reduced AVPU maintain their airway and consider placing in the recovery position.
- Minor head injuries can normally be treated at home with no need for further action and children do not need to stay awake if tired, just monitor them.
- If you are slightly concerned about the injury you can ring 111 for advice or take the patient to ED yourself.
- If they are taking any anticoagulant medication and suffered trauma they should go to ED.
- If you are not sure or worried don't hesitate to ring 999/112 for advice.

For further advice please go to https://www.headway.org.uk/

Trauma - Eye Injury

Eye injuries can be caused by various things such as: Trauma, burns, chemicals, blast, smoke, high intensity light and objects such as sand or dirt.

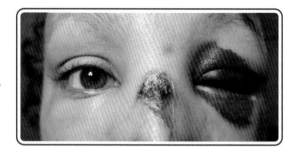

Treatment:

- Try and stop the person rubbing their eye.
- Don gloves if available, inspect the eye for contamination, rise with clean water or eye wash as required by tilting the persons head to the side with the bad eye down to ensure cleaning solution does not enter the good eye.
- For chemicals refer to safety data sheet which might suggest a buffer solution as eye wash.
- If there is something lodged in the eye, DO NOT attempt to remove it, try and pack around the eye socket but avoid applying pressure.
- A cold compress can help to reduce swelling and help with pain relief.
- Cover the injured eye with a clean eye pad or wound dressing avoiding any pressure.
- Closing the uninjured eye can reduce the risk of movement of the injured eye.
- If you are concerned about the injury ring 111 for advice or take the patient to MIU yourself.

Trauma - Knocked Out Teeth (Avulsed)

Time is important in the survival of a tooth. Research showed if the tooth is replaced into the socket within five minutes, it is likely to survive. However if the tooth is dry for more than 15 minutes, it's much less likely to be saved.

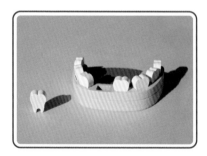

Treatment:

- Don gloves if available, pick up the tooth by the crown (the chewing surface) NOT the root.
- If dirty, gently rinse the tooth with water, but do not flush as we need to try and maintain the bacteria on the surface of the tooth.
- If possible reposition the tooth in the socket immediately and get person to gently bite on something soft.
- If you can't replace, keep the tooth moist by placing in milk within five minutes of being knocked out, this helps protect the tooth's own bacteria and the tooth's root's cells can survive for **30-60 minutes.**
- Get person to their dentist or ED within 30 minutes of the injury.

Trauma - Bleeding or Broken Nose

Bleeding from the nose can be caused by injury, high blood pressure our leaking blood vessels in the nose.

Signs and Symptoms:

- History of trauma to nose.
- Pain, swelling and redness.
- A crunching or crackling sound when they touch their nose.
- Difficulty breathing through their nose, feels blocked.
- Their nose has changed shape
- Sudden onset of nose bleed without trauma.

Treatment:

- Sit patient down with head tilting forward.
- Apply firm pressure on soft bit of nose just above nostrils for up to 15 minutes.
- Apply cold compress or cool pack to top of nose or back of neck.
- Treat any minor grazes or cuts.
- Do not try to straighten their nose if misaligned.

Go to hospital if they show any of the following:

- Nose bleed that won't stop especially if taking any blood thinning medication.
- Large cut or open wound on their nose or face, or something in the wound, such as glass.
- Clear, watery fluid trickling from their nose, could indicate a serious head injury.
- Severe headache with blurred or double vision.
- Eye pain and double vision.
- Neck pain or a stiff neck with numbness or tingling in their arms.

Trauma - Spinal Injury

You should always consider a spinal injury if the person has suffered an accident that could have directly affected their spine, including such things as: Fall from height, vehicle accident or severe head injury.

Signs and Symptoms:

- History of serious accident.
- Knocked unconscious.
- Complaining of severe pain in their neck or back.
- Complains of central neck pain on palpation.
- Unable to move their neck without pain.
- Feels weak or has pins and needles or numbness in limbs.
- Loss of sensation in limbs.
- Prioprizem in male casualty (erection).

Treatment:

- If the person is unconscious and you think they may have a spinal injury. Open airway and check breathing by placing your hands on either side of their head and use your fingertips to gently lift the angle of the jaw forward and upwards, without moving the head. Take care not to move the person's neck. But remember opening the airway takes priority over a neck injury. This is known as the jaw thrust technique (See page 13).
- If face down and you can't access their airway or check their breathing you need to move them onto their back using the face down to face up technique (See page 38).
- Otherwise don't move them unless in further danger.
- Reassure the person.
- Call 999/112 ask for Ambulance service.
- Ask person not to move and carry out a full top to toe secondary survey for other injuries.
- The best way to support their head and neck for a long time is to lie behind their head, rest your elbows on the ground, hold each side of their head with spread fingers careful not to cover their ears.
- Keep them warm and insulate from ground if possible to reduce the chance of Hypothermia.
- Continue to monitor their breathing and response level whilst supporting their head and neck until Ambulance arrives.
- If required turn them into the recovery position using the log roll technique (See page 37) or the single person spinal recovery position (See page 36).

Trauma - Chest Injury

An injury to the chest can be life threatening and could lead to a collapsed lung, broken or bruised ribs, flail chest or internal bleeding in your lungs, liver or spleen.

Signs and Symptoms:

- History of trauma.
- Pain in their chest area, particularly when they breathe in.
- Swelling, tenderness or bruising around the affected area.
- Feeling or hearing a crack if they break a rib.
- Having shortness of breath that's getting worse.
- Cyanosis grey/blue lips and skin, harder to see on dark skin.
- Unequal rise and fall of the chest.
- Pain in their stomach or shoulder.
- Coughing up blood.

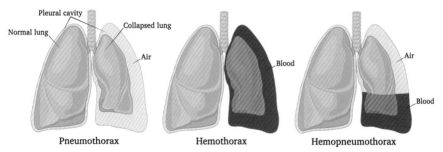

Pneumothorax   Hemothorax   Hemopneumothorax

Treatment:

- If they are conscious, if possibly sit them down but keep sat upright leaning towards the injured side, to help with breathing.
- Call 999/112 for ambulance service.
- Reassure the person.
- Control any Bleeding.
- Keep them warm.
- For an open chest wound, only cover if you have a chest seal dressing which would require extra training, best practice for First Aiders is to leave a wound open to fresh air however if bleeding direct pressure can be apply to the sides of the wound, care should be taken not to close the wound.
- Placing the arm on the injured side into an elevated sling can help with pain relief (See page 88).
- If they are unconscious and breathing, they can be placed in the recovery position with the injured side down.
- If not breathing or unsure Ring 999/112 back and start resuscitation.

Trauma – Internal Bleeding

Internal bleeding is normally caused by trauma. It can be a life threatening condition if not identified and treated quickly. The key areas of concern are head (See pages 76-77), chest (See page 81) and especially the abdomen where the liver and spleen are at high risk during trauma.

Signs and Symptoms:

- Abdominal pain or tight abdomen (Guarding) especially on palpation.
- Headache consider head injury (See pages 76-77).
- Chest pain or shortness of breath consider chest injury (See page 81).
- Cyanosis grey/blue lips and skin, harder to see on dark skin.
- Bruising or swelling.
- Confusion and memory loss.
- Nausea and vomiting.
- Heavy sweating and rapid pulse.

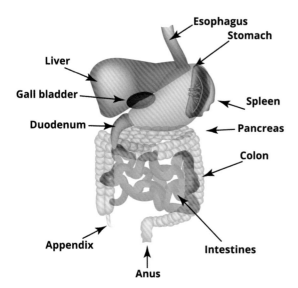

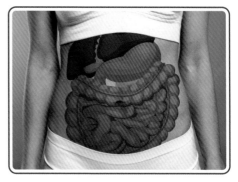

Treatment:

- Good primary and secondary surveys are key to identifying possible internal bleeding.
- Treat for shock, lie them down raise their legs and keep them warm (See pages 32-33).
- Call 999/112 for an Ambulance.
- If they are taking any anticoagulant medication and suffered trauma they should go to ED due to the higher risk of their blood not clotting.

Trauma - Abdominal Wound

Abdominal Distension - Suggests blood, fluid, intestinal perforation or acute gastric distension.

Abdominal Tenderness - Suggests injury, especially if over the liver or spleen.

Children with a history of significant trauma or high impact trauma should be admitted for observation even in the absence of examination findings

Children are different as their abdominal organs are relatively susceptible to injury because:

- The relatively small size of the patient allows a single impact to injure multiple organ systems.
- The abdominal wall is relatively thin (less muscle & less subcutaneous fat), so it provides less protection.
- The ribs are more pliable, providing less protection.
- The liver and spleen take up a larger proportion of the abdominal cavity.
- The diaphragm is more horizontal, tending to push the liver and spleen lower below the rib cage.
- The bladder in babies is an intra-abdominal organ.
- Adult protection systems, such as seat belts, are often ill fitting or worn incorrectly, causing deceleration injuries to the upper abdomen.

Treatment:

- Place the casualty in a comfortable position, preferably on their back with their knees flexed to relax the abdominal muscles and ease the pain.
- If the flexing of the knees opens the wound more then re-straighten the legs as required to put less stress on the wound site.
- Don gloves if available, cover the wound with a moist dressing or clean cloth.
- If no organs protruding cover wound with dressing or clean cloth, apply firm pressure and if necessary, hold the wound edges together to control bleeding.
- If organs are protruding do not touch any exposed organs with your hands due to the high risk of infection and do not apply direct pressure to protruding organs.
- If an organ is lying on the ground, use a moist dressing or clean cloth to gently pick up the organ and place the organ on top of the casualty's abdomen.
- Exposed organs that are not bleeding can be covered with cling film which may help reduce infection.
- Abdominal wounds are serious so call 999/112 for an Ambulance.

Trauma - Sprains, Strains and Fractures

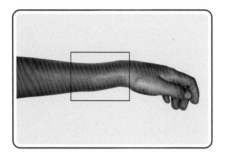
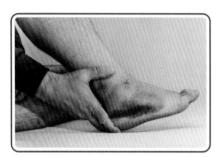

It is very difficult for a first aider to decide between a Sprain, Strain or Fracture, so if you're not sure they should go to hospital for an X-Ray (Most minor injury units can provide X-Rays)

A **Sprain** is an injury to the **ligaments around a joint**. Ligaments are strong, flexible fibres that hold bones together. When a ligament is stretched too far or tears, the joint will become painful and swell.

A **Strain** is an injury to a **Muscle or a Tendon**, the fibrous tissue that connects muscles to bone. Minor injuries may only overstretch a muscle or tendon, while more severe injuries may involve partial or complete tears in these tissues

A **Fracture** is break of any size to a bone. If the broken bone punctures the skin, it is called an **OPEN FRACTURE**, if not open to the air it is called a **CLOSED FRACTURE**, if it damages other parts like arteries it would be called a **COMPLICATED FRACTURE**, we can also get **STRESS FRACTURES** because of repeated or prolonged forces against the bone and lastly children younger than 10 can get **GREEN STICK FRACTURES** as their bones are still soft.

A **GREEN STICK FRACTURE** occurs when a bone bends and cracks, instead of breaking completely into separate pieces. It looks similar to what happens when you try to break a small, "green" branch on a tree.

A **BROKEN COLLARBONE**, or **FRACTURED CLAVICLE**, is a common injury when falls are involved; the collarbone is a long, slender bone that runs from the breastbone to each shoulder.

Signs and Symptoms of a Fracture, Sprain or Strain:

- Pain on impact or on palpation.
- Swelling.
- Bruising.
- Unable to weight bear.
- Misaligned or odd angle.
- Unable to move.
- Numbness, Tingling or Pins and Needles.
- Pale clammy skin, harder to see on dark skin check their tongue.
- Bone protruding out through skin or you feel a solid lump under skin (Tenting).
- Fingers or toes look blue, harder to see on dark skin
- Snapping or grinding noise (Crepitus).
- Affected leg is shorter than the other leg.

Typical Bone Fractures

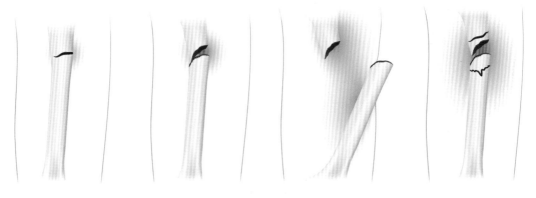

| Greenstick | Closed | Open | Complicated |

Treatment of Fractures:

- Treat any bleeding (See page 73-75).
- Cover any protruding bones, pack round with dressings as required (See page 91).
- Sit or lie the person down, consider shock and keep warm.
- Gently hold a cool pack or a bag of frozen peas wrapped in a towel on the area for 15 to 20 minutes.
- Remove any jewellery or loosen tight clothing and remove shoes or boots as required.
- Check capillary refill on fingers or toes as required.
- Don't give anything to eat or drink in case they need surgery.
- In remote environments consider leg splinting (Covered on Outdoor First Aid Course).
- Consider applying a sling for arm injuries as required. (See pages 87-88)
- For serious injuries call 999/112 for Ambulance.
- For less serious injuries get person to MIU or ED.
- Remember if using a Sling, Nose to Toes and Point to Joint.

Treatment for Sprains and Strains (Rest Ice Comfortable Support Elevate):

- Sit person down and get them to rest.
- Consider gently holding a cool pack or a bag of frozen peas wrapped in a towel on the area for 15 to 20 minutes every 2 to 3 hours. However, some recent research suggests not cooling sports injuries due to the effect it might have on the healing process.
- If they are wearing a shoe or boot best to consider removal depending on environment.
- Elevate the injury if possible.
- Compression bandage is no longer recommended, just comfortable support.
- Consider shock and keep warm.
- If the injury is not better in three days it may require an X-Ray.

Trauma - Dislocations

Dislocations can be very painful and can temporarily deform and immobilise a joint. Most common are shoulders and fingers, but can affect elbows, knees and hips.

Signs and Symptoms:

- Swelling and bruising around the joint.
- It may look shorter, bent or deformed.
- Complain of a severe, sickening pain.
- Unable to move the joint.

Treatment:

- Do not attempt to replace as this can damage blood vessels, muscles, ligaments and nerves.
- Use a cool pack covered in a cloth around the joint to help reduce swelling and pain.
- Support with sling as required.
- Fingers can be protected by strapping the injured finger to the finger next to it.
- For serious injuries call 999/112 for Ambulance.
- For less serious injuries get person to MIU or ED.

Support Sling (Can be used for Upper Arm, Forearm, Shoulder and Wrist Injuries)

Hold sling as shown, 1 to top(nose). 2 to bottom (toes). 3 to elbow of injured arm (Point to joint) then lay over the top of arm.

Place sling under arm as shown with care.

Tying a knot at point 3 before applying can help with support.

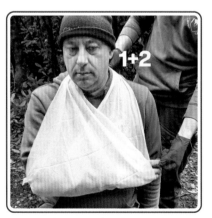

Tie point 1 to point 2 with a simple reef knot just on shoulder away from bones. Check capillary blood flow.

Elevated Sling (Can be used for Chest and Hand Injuries)

Hold sling as shown, 1 to top (Nose). 2 to bottom (Toes). 3 to elbow of injured arm (Point to joint) then lay over the top of arm.

Tuck remaining sling under arm in a scooping movement, point 1 should be over the shoulder.

Gather up the spare material at point 3 and twist material towards the back at least twice.

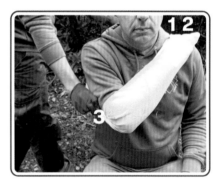

Take point 2 round the back under shoulder and meet point 1.

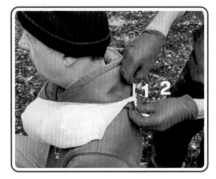

Tie point 1 to point 2 with a simple reef knot just on shoulder away from bones.

The thumb can be taken out to check capillary blood flow if required.

Trauma - Bruising

A bruise (Haematoma) forms due to bleeding under intact skin. It usually occurs as a result of accidental trauma, but non-accidental bruising is the most common injury sustained by children who have been subject to physical abuse. Also the congenital birth mark **"Mongolian Blue Spot"** found most commonly in African or Asian ethnic backgrounds can present like bruising. Also certain medications increase the chance of bruising especially anticoagulant medication such as Warfarin.

Treatment:

- Good history taking is essential to establish possible cause.
- Good secondary survey for other injuries especially fractures or internal bleeding.
- Applying a cold compress to the injured area can help reduce pain and any swelling.
- Monitor for other injury signs and symptoms.
- If you have any concern for the origin of injury especially in children or vulnerable adults consider contacting 111 or taking to MIU for further advise especially around safeguarding.
- If they are taking any anticoagulant medication and suffered trauma they should go to ED.

Trauma - Graze

This is normally a wound which only effects the top layer of skin and is classed as a minor injury. However the risk of infection should not be underestimated.

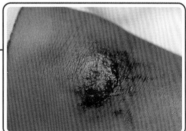

Treatment:

- Wash your hands thoroughly and dry them if possible.
- Don PPE as required.
- Clean the wound with bottled or tap water, eye wash or saline wipes. (Avoid alcohol wipes if possible).
- Pat the area dry using a gauze swab.
- Apply a plaster or low adherent dressing with conforming bandaged for larger wounds.
- Air drying is not now recommended as it may increase the healing time.
- Keeping the wound covered with a clean dressing, changed regularly should improve healing time and further reduce infection risk.
- Seek medical advice if wound becomes red, hot or starts producing pus, consider sepsis (See page 62-63).

Trauma - Embedded Object

We should consider an object embedded if removing it would lead to more tissue damage, severe external bleeding or any increase in internal bleeding. However small splinters and thorns would be classed as minor embedded objects which can be safely removed.

Treatment of Splinters, Thorns and Small Fishing Hooks:

- Don PPE as required.
- Clean the surrounding are with soap and water or saline.
- Using clean tweezers grip the object as close to the skin as possible. If the object is too deep to get a firm grip consider MIU.
- Draw the object out as straight as possible at the same angle as it went in.
- Be careful to dispose of the object safely.
- Gently squeeze the wound to encourage slight bleeding to help flush the wound.
- Clean wound with soap and water or saline and cover with plaster or dressing as required.
- Small fishing hooks can be removed in a similar way but you need to snip off the barb end first and remove it the same way it went in.
- Research shows that applying an even layer Magnesium Sulphate Paste over an embedded splinter or especially a thorn, then covering with a plaster can help to remove the object over a couple of days.
- For safe Tick removal (See pages 100-101).

Clean around splinter

Pull straight out

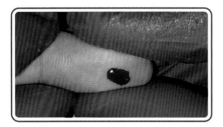

Encourage bleeding

Clean and dress wound

Treatment of Large Embedded Object:

- Do not remove large embedded objects or a person from an impalement because they may be plugging the wound and restricting bleeding.
- Place a still rolled up dressing either side of object and apply even pressure, squeezing the pads around the object and secure them in place with a conforming bandage.
- Use a similar procedure for a fractured bone that is protruding through skin, also cover the end of any bone with clean dressing to reduce the chance of infection.
- Treat for shock (See pages 32-33).
- For large embedded objects or impalement ring 999/112 and ask for Fire Service, followed by the Ambulance Service.
- If the object has been removed this would now be a PUNCTURE WOUND. If in the lungs treat as chest injury (See page 81) if another part of body treat as for bleeding (See pages 72-75).

Treatment Objects in Other Orifices:

Nose

- Ask person to tell you what's stuck up there, if they can.
- Most objects are not immediately serious, however button batteries or anything containing toxic chemicals can cause serious damage in a matter of hours if not removed so ring 111 or take to MIU for further advice.
- You can try the "mother's kiss" method, which works best for small, hard objects like beads. Use your finger to plug the persons clear nostril, place your mouth over their mouth, then blow gently. The force of your breath might be enough to force the object out.

Ear

- Do not try to remove the object as this can make their ear sore and painful, which will make a child less likely to cooperate when a healthcare professional later tries to remove the object.
- Ring GP, 111 or take too MIU.
- For a suspected insect in an ear, lay them on their side with the affected ear facing up, try either pouring saline solution, warm mineral oil or vegetable oil in the ear until it's full, wait five to ten minutes to ensure the bug or larvae has died, then gently turn their head and let the oil seep out.

For all other orifices consider MIU.

Trauma - Crush Injury

When a body is crushed between two objects, muscle cells begin to die almost instantaneously within the body caused by **Lysis** (the breakdown of a cell membrane) **Ischemia** (reduction of oxygen to the tissue), and **Vascular Compromise** (reduced blood flow). This will increase toxin levels in the blood.

If the blood flow is restricted or impaired for more than 15 minutes, these toxins, if released into the rest of the body, can cause organ damage. This process is called 'Crush Syndrome' and the patient is at a high risk of death.

Treatment:

- In 2001 The Faculty of Pre-Hospital Care stated "The patient should be released as quickly as possible, irrespective of the length of time trapped." However, The Voluntary Aid Societies in 2021 still recommend the following treatment.
- Conduct a primary and secondary survey.
- Establish how long the person has been crushed.
- Call 999/112 and asking for Fire Service.
- If less than 15 mins try and release the crush if safe to do so.
- Consider fitting a loose tourniquet to a limb if severe bleeding is suspected on release.
- Once clear only move patient as far as is required for treatment and to be safe.
- Re-do primary and secondary survey.
- If more than 15 mins do not release unless in further danger and wait for the Fire Service.
- Treat as best you can.

Trauma - Suspension Trauma

This normally occurs when anyone is held in an upright position with their legs immobile, such as when using a fall arrest system such as a harness. This can lead to lose of circulation, fainting and death and the longer they are suspended the worse the outcome might be. Any longer than 10 mins could start to affect a person.

Signs and Symptoms:

- Pallor (Skin looks lighter than normal, harder to see on darker skin).
- Sweating.
- Shortness of breath.
- Blurred vision.
- Dizziness.
- Nausea.
- Numbness of the legs.
- Unconsciousness.

Treatment:

- If person is unconscious, airway maintenance is the top priority.
- Rescue the person safely and as quickly as possible.
- If help required for rescue ring 999/112 and ask for Fire Service.
- Whilst waiting for help get person to pump their legs, try and provide limb support, get them to press their legs against a firm surface, like a tree, or at least try and keep their legs horizontal. This has been shown to reduce the chance of fainting.
- Once person on ground place in the recovery position and conduct a primary and secondary survey and treat any injuries.

In the United Kingdom and Australia, fall protection training programs recommend using the recovery position for treating suspension trauma symptoms. The recovery position involves laying the person on their side on the ground and positioning them so their head is tipped down. The concept behind this position is that when someone is lying on their side, they are able to let their body naturally re-balance without stressing the heart to work against gravity.

For further advice please go to: www.cureus.com/articles/32357-suspension-trauma-a-clinical-review

Trauma - Amputation

An amputation could be fully detached or still partially attached. It is normally caused by trauma and might not be easily identified due to clothing such as gloves or other PPE obstructing the view of the wound.

Treatment:

- Identify wound area immediately and don PPE as required.
- Stop any catastrophic haemorrhage (See pages 74-75).
- Treat any bleeding (See pages 72-73).
- If possible rinse any dirt from wound or partially amputated part with clean water or saline.
- For partially amputated wound cover with clean moist dressing if possible..
- Consider cleaning the amputated part with water or saline then wrap in a clean moist dressing, seal in a plastic bag or clingfilm, then keep cool by surrounding with cool packs or ice in a separate bag. It is important the ice does not touch the amputated part.
- Treat for shock (See pages 32-33).
- For minor amputations transport to ED, for large amputations or you are not sure ring 999/112.

Trauma - Avulsion or De-gloving

An avulsion injury extends through all the layers of skin and normally leaves a flap of tissue that is still connected. If the tissue is completely detached treat as an amputated part see above.

An avulsion that wraps all the way around an extremity and causes the layers of tissue to pull away is called a **Degloving** injury. Imagine peeling a glove off your hand so that it ends up inside-out. That's where the term comes from.

Degloving can affect any part of the body, such as the fingers, feet, or hands. A common cause of degloving injury is when a ring catches on something, resulting in a degloving injury of the finger.

Treatment:

- Treat as amputation above.
- If the tissue (skin, fat, and muscle) is not completely torn away, wash away any dirt with clean water or saline solution and replace the flap, then cover the wound with a clean moist dressing and transport to ED.

Trauma - Animal or Human Bite

Humans and animals have lots of bacteria in their mouths, which can cause an infection like sepsis if a bite breaks the skin. These infections are rarely serious if treated quickly, but occasionally they can spread to the blood or other parts of the body. Serious infections such as tetanus and rabies are extremely rare in the UK, but it's important to get serious bites looked at as treatment to prevent these infections may be required, especially human bites which can present a higher risk of infection.

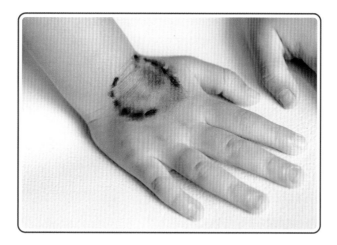

Treatment:

- Remove further animal danger.
- Don PPE as required.
- Clean area with soap and water or saline to help remove bacteria even if the skin doesn't appear to be broken.
- Remove any none embedded objects from the bite, such as teeth, hair or dirt.
- Encourage the wound to bleed slightly by gently squeezing it, unless it's already bleeding freely.
- Treat the wound as per instructions on pages 72-73.
- Consider sepsis (See pages 62-63).
- If the bite has severed a body part like a finger or ear, following guidance for amputation on opposite page 94.
- If you are concerned about the injury ring 111 for advice or take the patient to MIU yourself.
- For large animal bites don't hesitate to ring 999/112 for advice.

Snake Bite (Adder)

The Adder is the only native venomous snake in the UK and is responsible for around 70-100 bites a year with the majority of bites occurring between April and September, with a marked peak in July-August. However in about 70% of bites there is a negligible reaction. Although some effects are very unpleasant they are easily treated.

That said these bites are potentially very serious and should not be under-estimated as in a small proportion of cases they can lead to severe effects requiring extensive hospital treatment.

Thankfully Human fatalities are exceptionally rare in the UK with 14 recorded human deaths since 1876, the last being in 1975. In recent decades there have been a number of life-threatening adder bites. However advances in medical care have made a significant impact on outcomes.

Signs and Symptoms:

- Severe pain at the location of the bite.
- Visible double puncture wound.
- Dizziness or fainting due to shock.
- Swelling, redness and bruising at the location of the bite.
- Nausea and vomiting.
- Itchy lumps on the skin.
- Swelling of the lips, tongue, gums and throat.
- Breathing difficulties.
- Confusion.
- Irregular heartbeat.

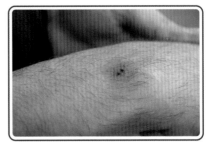

Snake Bite

Female Adder

Male Adder

Treatment:

- Stay calm, don't panic and try to remember the shape, size and colour of the snake.
- Keep the patient as still as possible with no walking to prevent the venom spreading around their body.
- Keep a close eye on person for Signs and Symptoms of Anaphylaxis (See pages 40-41).
- Young children should be carried.
- Keeping the bitten area lower than the heart can help, so sitting up might be best.
- Remove jewellery and watches from the bitten limb as they could cut into your skin if the limb swells.
- Irrigate the bite area with fresh water to remove any venom from skin.
- A cold compress of bandage or other material soaked in cool water might help limit the spread of the venom and relieve any pain (Not cool packs).
- Loosen tight clothing if possible.
- Do not leave on their own if possible.
- Seek immediate medical attention ring 999/112 or take straight to ED.
- If they become unresponsive conduct primary survey, if breathing normally consider recovery position.
- If not breathing or unsure Ring 999/112 back and start resuscitation.

The following are not recommended:

- Trying to suck the venom out of the bite.
- Trying to cut the venom out of the bite or make it bleed.
- Rubbing anything into the wound or apply ice, heat or chemicals.
- Putting anything around the bitten limb to stop the spread of venom (such as a tight pressure band, tourniquet or ligature) as it won't help, and can cause swelling or make it worse; it could also damage the limb, leading to the need for amputation.
- Trying to catch or kill the snake. (They are protected in law).
- They may be admitted to hospital so the bite can be assessed and their condition closely monitored.

For more info visit NHS website www.nhs.uk/conditions/snake-bites

Bee and Wasp Stings

Bees and Wasps are very common in the UK, with wasps being more prevalent from Apr till Oct. Bees are very gentle and rarely sting as it normally causes their death as they leave their stinger behind, whereas wasps can be more aggressive and sting at random and don't leave a stinger behind.

Signs and Symptoms:

- Pain at site of sting.
- Puncture mark at site of sting.
- Swelling at site of sting, especially in mouth or face which could lead to a swollen face, mouth or throat.
- Fast heart rate.
- Dizziness or feeling faint.
- Feeling sick or vomiting.
- Difficulty in breathing with possible wheezing.

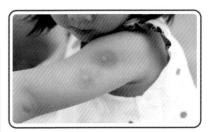

Treatment:

- Keep a close eye on person for Signs and Symptoms of Anaphylaxis (See pages 40-41).
- Remove any Bee stinger left behind as soon as possible to prevent any more venom being released, by scraping it out sideways with something with a hard edge, such as a bank card or fingernails.
- Do not pinch the sting with your fingers or tweezers because you may spread the venom.
- Consider traditional home remedies such as (A paste of Bicarbonate of Soda for BEES) and (A Vinegar-soaked dressing for WASPS) which may help reduce the pain if applied quickly.
- Remove any jewellery from sting area to reduce the impact of any swelling.
- Bee and Wasp stings may also respond well to bite creams containing antihistamine.
- Apply a cold compress (such as a flannel or cloth cooled with cold water) or a cool pack to any swelling for at least 10 minutes.
- Avoid scratching the area or bursting any blisters to reduce the risk of infection, covering with a clean dressing can help.

Bee

Bee Sting

Wasp

Treatment of other Insect Bites:

There are lots of other insects in the UK that can cause bites, most common are Mosquitoes and Horseflies less common are Spiders and Blandford Fly.
Also contact with Caterpillar hairs can cause a reaction.

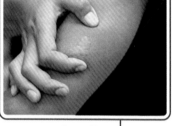
Insect Bite

- Remove Caterpillar hairs from skin using water or sticky tape.
- Wash the affected area with soap and water.
- Apply a cold compress (such as a flannel or cloth cooled with cold water) or a cool pack to any swelling for at least 10 minutes.
- Raise or elevate the affected area if possible, as this can help reduce swelling (only to heart height).
- Avoid scratching the area or bursting any blisters to reduce the risk of infection, covering with a clean dressing or pla ster can help.
- Most bites will respond well to bite creams containing antihistamine, however should be avoided for Blandford Fly and Caterpillar hairs.
- The pain, swelling and itchiness can sometimes last a few days.
- A Cleg (Horse Fly) bite can cause some people to experience dizziness, weakness, wheezing or something called angio-oedema – itchy, pink or red swellings around the eyes or lips.
- A good tip would be to monitor redness and mark it with a pen, if the redness spreads beyond original marking it could be a sign of infection so seek medical advice.

Cleg or Horse Fly

Mosquito

Tick Bite

Your main aim is to remove all parts of the tick's body promptly, preventing it regurgitating its stomach contents into your bite wound as Ticks can carry diseases like Lyme Disease or Encephalitis Virus.

Lyme Disease is a bacterial infection that can be spread to humans by infected ticks with symptoms typically developing 3 to 30 days after a bite from an infected tick.

Encephalitis Virus (TBEV) is a viral infection that spreads through tick bites and can cause a range of diseases, from mild flu-like illness, all the way to severe infection in the central nervous system such as meningitis or encephalitis (swelling of the brain).

Signs and Symptoms of Tick-Borne Lyme Disease:

- Possible bulls eye rash.
  (however not everyone gets a rash).
- Flu-like symptoms.
- High temperature.
- Feeling hot and shivery.
- Headaches.
- Muscle and joint pain.
- Tiredness and loss of energy.

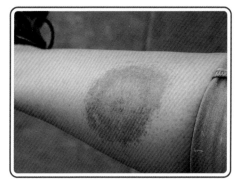

Signs and Symptoms of Tick-Borne Encephalitis Virus (TBEV):

- High temperature.
- Headache.
- Neck stiffness.
- Confusion.
- Seizures or fits.
- Stroke like symptoms
  (See pages 52-53).
- Reduced or loss of consciousness.
- Seek urgent medical attention if anyone is experiencing the above symptoms.

Treatment:

- Don PPE if possible as the tick may contain potentially infected blood.

- Remove Tick as soon as possible using a tick removal tool like a tick card, tick tong or special tick tweezers and follow the instructions provided.

- Two common types of removal tool available are illustrated below; these tools will grip the head of the tick without squashing the body.

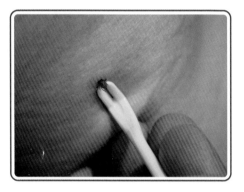

Tick Tong

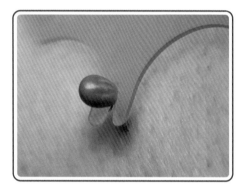

Tick Card

- After you have removed the tick, dispose of it safely or keep it in a sealed container and consider sending it to Public Health England's Tick Surveillance Scheme. https://www.gov.uk/guidance/tick-surveillance-scheme.

- Thoroughly cleanse the bite site, the tool and your hands with soap and water after removal as they may contain potentially infected blood.

- Twisting or grabbing the tick with tool or fingers is no longer recommended as this may break the tick and leave the head in place and increase the infection risk due to regurgitated infected blood.

- Burning the tick off, apply petroleum jelly, nail polish or any other chemical is not recommended.

Weever Fish Sting

There are two species of venomous weever fish in the UK, they can be between 8 to 30 cm in length and are common during the warm summer months, where they come inshore and can be found in very shallow water or buried in sand, leaving their poisonous dorsal spines sticking out injecting a painful venom into any unsuspecting victim who stands on them. Sadly there is no anti-venom for the toxin.

Signs and Symptoms:

- Severe pain around the area of the sting, worst around 30 minutes from the sting, then gradually subsides.
- Visual embedded spine.
- Swelling around the area.
- Itching.
- Numbness.
- Headache.
- Joint aches.
- Occasionally vomiting.
- Light headedness and fainting.
- Breathing difficulties.
- Possible anaphylaxis (See pages 40-41).

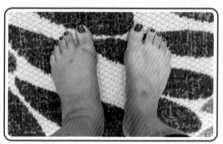

Treatment:

- Remove patient from water.
- Sit patient down.
- Check for spines and remove with tweezers or scrape out immediately.
- Keep a close eye on person for Signs and Symptoms of Anaphylaxis (See pages 40-41).
- Find a source of hot water. If you're on the beach, go to the lifeguard station as soon as possible, they should have access to hot water. The water needs to be as hot as the person can bear, but still comfortable enough to place the effected part into for 30 to 90 minutes. This has been shown to reduce the effectiveness of the venom by breaking down its protein, and it may help reduce pain.
- Clean any wound with soap and water.
- Keep any wound open and let it bleed as this will help clear the body of some of the toxins.
- If you are concerned about the sting ring 111 for advice or take the patient to MIU yourself.

Jellyfish Stings

Although around six species of Jellyfish can be found in UK waters they are not dangerous. However stings from the Portuguese Man O'War, Lion's Mane and Compass Jellyfish can be painful and those who have allergic reactions to stings should be monitored and seek medical attention if necessary.

Signs and Symptoms:

- Burning, prickling and stinging pain that can radiate up a leg or an arm.
- Welts or tracks on the skin like a print of the tentacles that contacted the skin.
- Itchiness.
- Swelling.

A 2017 study found that the following treatment can reduce the pain of Jellyfish stings. The study looked specifically at Lion's Mane Jellyfish, which have large tentacles, causing very painful stings.

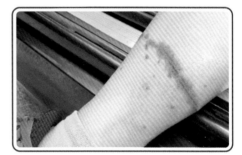

Treatment:

- Thoroughly rinse the affected area with vinegar or with a commercial spray if available.
- Remove the tentacles while still rinsing using tweezers or scraping with credit card. The tentacles can keep stinging as long as they are in contact with skin, so wear gloves or put plastic bags on the hands.
- Keep a close eye on person for Signs and Symptoms of Anaphylaxis (See pages 40-41).
- Apply a heat pack or immerse the affected area in water of a temperature at least (45°C) for up to 40 minutes, cold water can make tentacles release more venom.
- After being stung, patient should stay out of the water for the rest of the day, as salt water may make the pain worse and there are likely to be other jellyfish in the area.
- When a jellyfish tentacle punctures the skin and draws blood, the open wound can become infected so patient should go to MIU or ED within a few hours.

Trauma - Burns and Scalds

Superficial – Only burns the outer layer of skin, common from hot water on sun burn, indication red skin, feels tight with pain.

Partial Thickness – This burns through two layers, the Epidermis and the Dermis, indication is normally blisters. Red skin around edges, swelling, blisters and pain.

Full Thickness – The worst type of burn, can go deep into the Subcutaneous layer. Skin is open, nerves are killed causing less pain in the middle. However, can be very painful around the edges. Common in electrical burns as it enters or leaves the body.

Electrical Burn – Can cause all of the above, always check for an exit burn, this can cause internal tissue damage.

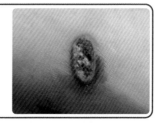

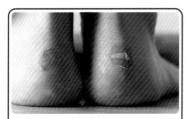

Blister Burn – Normally caused by friction, presents as superficial or partial thickness, if blisters burst infection is a high risk.

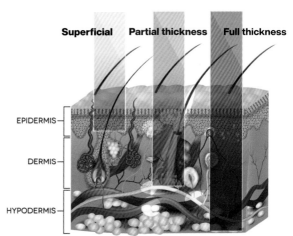

Superficial   Partial thickness   Full thickness

EPIDERMIS

DERMIS

HYPODERMIS

Treatment of Burns:

- Remove the cause, if electrical make sure power is isolated.
- Cool the burn as quickly as possible with cool running water for a minimum of **20 minutes**, longer if redness and pain is still present.
- If water is not immediately available cover with a burns dressing if available and cling film, then seek medical help, you should aim to apply water within at least three hours. If limited water available, apply a cool water soaked compress using any clean wetted lint free material.
- While cooling the burn carefully remove any clothing that is not attached to the skin, as this is a barrier to cooling. Also remove jewellery in case of swelling.
- If you're cooling a large burnt area, particularly in babies, children and elderly people, be aware that it may cause hypothermia (it may be necessary to stop cooling the burn to avoid hypothermia).
- If dealing with a burn from sugar such as hot toffee or marshmallow, cool water can make it stick more, so you may need to use warm water to remove before cooling.
- If dealing with small blisters, special blister plasters are available and can be very effective.
- If the burn has cooled, cover it loosely with cling film. If cling film isn't available, cover with a clean none adherent dressing, lint free wet material or burns dressing.
- Do not wrap the burn tightly as swelling may lead to further injury and do not apply creams, lotions or sprays to the burn.
- Burn area is calculated in percentage with the persons hand being around 1% of their body, for burns larger than 1% medical help should be sought by either going to MIU or calling 999/112.

1%

Treatment of Chemical Burns:

- Consult COSHH Safety Data Sheet to ensure it is ok to cool with water or a specific chemical antidote may be available and wear PPE as required.
- Cool the burn with cool running water or a recommended buffer solution for at least **20 minutes**, try to ensure the chemical has been fully removed from the affected area.
- If chemical or Acid is affecting the face, lean the person forward and poor water over their head, this will run round the face and keep the airway clear.
- If the chemical has been swallowed and may cause burning, get person to rinse mouth with water and sip cool water to help reduce the burning of the upper airway and oesophagus. Milk Is not recommended due to the increased risk of vomiting.
- If unsure seek medical advice ring 111 or 999/112.

For further information, please go to www.brittishburnassociation.org

Poisoning

Causes of poisoning can include:

- Contact with chemicals.
- An overdose of drugs or medicine.
- Eating something like wild plants or fungi.
- Alcohol poisoning.
- Carbon Monoxide inhalation.
- Smoke inhalation.

Drug Overdose

Opioids or narcotics such as Morphine, Heroin, Codeine and Methadone can cause pupils to constrict.

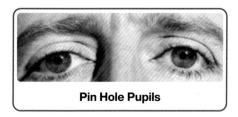

Pin Hole Pupils

Cocaine, Ecstasy (MDMA), LSD, Marijuana can cause pupils to dilate.

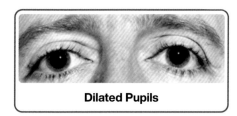

Dilated Pupils

Signs and Symptoms:

- Vomiting.
- Stomach pain.
- Burns or burning sensation in mouth or throat.
- Confusion.
- Drowsiness.
- Unconsciousness.
- Seizures.

Treatment:

- Try and identify the cause of poisoning.
- Do not expose yourself to the agent, consider PPE and fresh air as required.
- Do not give anything to eat or drink unless a healthcare professional advises you to.
- Do not try to cause vomiting unless a healthcare professional advises you to due to toxic substance.
- If they have swallowed a corrosive substance treat as for burns (See page 105).
- Stay with the person, as their condition may get worse and they could become unconscious.
- For suspected chemical poisoning follow the instruction on Safety Data Sheet.
- If CPR is required care should be taken when giving mouth-to-mouth.

Alcohol Poisoning

Signs and Symptoms:

- Confusion.
- Vomiting.
- Seizures.
- Slow breathing, which is fewer than eight breaths a minute.
- Skin becoming pale, blue and grey which can be harder to see on dark skin.
- Low body temperature, also known as hypothermia.
- Trouble staying conscious or awake.

Treatment:

- If you suspect Alcohol Poisoning you should ring 999/112.
- Maintain patient's airway, consider recovery position.
- Keep patient warm.
- Monitor.

Notes